the

FLOWER HUNTER

the
FLOWER HUNTER

*Seasonal flowers inspired by nature
and gathered from the garden*

LUCY HUNTER

RYLAND PETERS & SMALL
LONDON • NEW YORK

For the husband and teenager, who always make me smile.

ART DIRECTOR
Leslie Harrington

SENIOR COMMISSIONING
EDITOR
Annabel Morgan

HEAD OF PRODUCTION
Patricia Harrington

PUBLISHER
Cindy Richards

INDEXER
Hilary Bird

All photography by Lucy Hunter,
except page 36 Max Gill and
page 37 Ben Wall.

First published in 2021 by
Ryland Peters & Small
20–21 Jockey's Fields,
London WC1R 4BW
and
341 E 116th St
New York, NY 10029
www.rylandpeters.com

Text and photography © Lucy
Hunter 2021.
Design © Ryland Peters & Small
2021

ISBN 978-1-78879-384-1

Printed and bound in China
10 9 8 7 6 5 4

Contents

INTRODUCTION

I GREW UP ON THE OUTSKIRTS OF SOUTH-EAST LONDON,
ON A WIDE, TREE-LINED AVENUE OF CLOSELY PACKED SEMI-
DETACHED EDWARDIAN HOUSES.

My parents weren't gardeners, but we had a good-sized lawn
and I spent all the time I could up in a tree house that Dad made
with old planks. My sister Sylvie and I rigged up a pulley system
with a bucket on a piece of rope between two trees, and I seem
to recall us spending a lot of time pulling it back and forth. I
can't for the life of me remember what we put in the bucket.
I'd like to think it was something fabulous, like a bunch of wild
grasses tied with a faded silk ribbon, but it was probably just a
couple of muddy stones. Eventually, Sylvie would get bored and
return to the house to practise her ballet, but I revelled in the big
skies up in the trees, high above the busy and noisy city, even at
the age of seven.

THE RESTLESS CREATIVE
I've always found myself drawn to the landscape,
and if I'm not outside in it, then I'm painting or
gathering armfuls of it, whatever the season, and
bringing it inside. It keeps me forever curious and
quietens my restless mind (opposite).

My grandmother gardened in big floppy hats and flowing skirts. Her garden wasn't fashionable at a time of manicured lawns and well-behaved bedding plants, but to me it was a romantic wonder. There were overgrown rose bushes and tall shasta daisies in conversation with big, blowsy scarlet oriental poppies. She taught me to make patchwork quilts, and press flowers within the pages of old magazines. Time with her was time just to be and to explore. No pressure. No expectations.

At 18, I went to university to study fine art. I didn't have a plan, but at the time university was the unquestionable next step. My sense of worth was tied up in following the crowd. I wafted around with a paintbrush, covering my dungarees in paint splatters in an effort to resemble a serious artist, while struggling to find direction. I was missing the point, but it took me another 30 years to understand that.

I left university knowing that I needed to get a 'proper' job. My canvases and paint brushes were put in the attic, and I got a job in a bank. I got to wear a suit. I was busy! I was a success! And I hated it.

REAL FLOWERS

A sprawl of exuberant dahlias in the garden in late summer, just waiting to be cut (above). They don't all stand straight or grow to the same height; some have weather-damaged petals, while others grow at strange angles. They may not be ideal for a commercial grower, but these dahlias grow as nature intended and are therefore perfect in my eyes. I am always trying to recreate that wild, utterly romantic and gloriously untamed corner of the garden in an urn, and so I deliberately seek out flowers that kink and curve, reach for the light yet have space to breathe, look relaxed and contented, and fill the house with scent and joy (opposite).

It was eight years before I realized there was more to life than high heels and trouser suits, and I left to forge a career for myself as a garden designer. I took on a few small projects, pored over books and learned plant names. My husband helped me dig up our back garden and plant flowers. I killed quite a few, but others grew like weeds. I learned as I went, and I loved it.

The tiny jobs led to new clients and, gradually, bigger and more complex projects. Slowly, though, my creativity was dwindling. I spent all hours studying spreadsheets, designing lighting plans and ordering paving. By the end of each project, I was all but burned out. I had become successful, I had won awards, but I had stopped being curious, stopped looking at flowers and plants in detail and wondering.

My sister offered me a lifeline. She and her partner asked me to design the flowers for their wedding. I threw myself into mastering the principles and mechanics of floristry, but I was disappointed with the commercial flowers on offer. I couldn't realize the romantic vision in my head using imported, scentless roses. I didn't want to use peonies in October. Rather, I wanted to embrace the seasons and recreate the romance and spontaneity of my grandmother's garden. So I taught myself, through trial and error, which flowers cut from the garden would look glorious in an urn or bouquet for 12 hours, and which are better left outside. I took workshops and learned from other florists that I admired, then set about crafting my own take on floral design, weaving it with my landscape design work. The two now inform each other.

We live in a busy world, but it never ceases to amaze me how the garden quietly gets on and does her own thing regardless. We need to take the time to look at, marvel and appreciate the splendour of the natural world. Whether you have a large garden, a small courtyard, a balcony or even just a window box, there will be a plant that you can sow, nurture, grow and, eventually, cut and bring inside to arrange in an urn or a vase or a glass jar. I can't express the enjoyment this process gives me, and I hope this book will spark some creative joy and inspire you to do the same.

SPRING

a season of optimism

'To accomplish great things, we must not
only act, but also dream, not only plan, but
also believe.' ANATOLE FRANCE

CONNECTING TO THE LANDSCAPE

BY THE TIME WINTER IS SLOWLY THINKING ABOUT LOOSENING HIS FROSTY GRIP ON OUR FROZEN SOIL AND MAKING MOVES TOWARDS THE SOUTHERN HEMISPHERE, I AM READY TO WELCOME SPRING LIKE A LONG-LOST FRIEND.

Desperate to ditch the scarves and hats that have given me a bad hair day for so long, I raid the wardrobe for anything that isn't thermal, itchy or insulated against the elements. I'm thinking of something light, perhaps even wafty. The sun streaming through the gaps in the clouds is warm and whispers of great things on the horizon. But a thin, wintry wind with long, icy fingers is still lurking around the corner and in the shade. He can turn a summer dream into a winter shiver, and he's not done with us just yet.

GLAMOROUS GRANNY
Aquilegia vulgaris (or granny's bonnet, as I've always known them) self-seed like crazy in the garden. In late spring, just as the bulbs are packing up their party frocks and the roses are thinking about their moment in the sun, the aquilegia dance like butterflies on long, thin stems above mounds of fresh green foliage (opposite).

The Garden

THERE IS A CHATTER IN THE AIR. The birds are making their nests under the eaves again and having very heated debates while doing it. The dawn chorus sounds like a football match. There is a woodpecker drilling a very large hole in a tree in the woods at the end of our garden. Well, we presume he's in the woods and not our eaves. That would be a bit concerning. The dogs seem to have turned into dressage ponies overnight. Wilson skips sideways across the lawn to inspect his mud hole, while the cats sniff the fresh spring air before rediscovering their joy at lying upside down on the new shoots that are appearing on the *Nepeta mussinii* (catmint), very happy indeed in their newly discovered herbal oblivion.

I take a cup of coffee, and squeeze my feet into a pair of wellies before opening the kitchen door and taking deep breaths of the smell of warming soil and freshly cut grass. I know how the animals feel. There

are shoots of life all around. The daffodil bulbs that we planted at the edges of the lawn in early autumn are making their first appearances, with tall green leaves and fat flower buds. The tulips in pots are just poking through the surface of the soil, the hellebores have hit their stride, covering the edges of the borders with their beautiful faces, and the bare branches of the cherry tree are about to burst into an explosion of pink blossom. I make my way towards the greenhouse, carefully avoiding the large mud hole where Wilson is admiring his collection of tennis balls and other bits of stolen treasure, and open the tin with the packets of seed stored inside. Soon, I think, soon. My greenhouse

SPRING FORWARD

After the long, cold winter months, surely there is no more welcome sight than a carpet of narcissus stretching as far as the eye can see. This meadow of narcissus bursting into flower beneath blossoming magnolia trees is at Bodnant Garden in North Wales, cared for by the National Trust (above).

isn't heated, so when the nights aren't quite so cold and the daytime temperature reaches around 20°C/68°F behind the glass, I will sow most of the annuals that will fill my cutting garden with scent and delight during the summer months.

In the meantime, I bring in the pots of tiny daffodils, muscari and fritillary bulbs that I potted up in autumn and place them on a sunny windowsill. With a little warmth, they will flower early and give me much-needed inspiration before the garden catches up. Once they have flowered, I will plant the bulbs in the garden. I need to cut down the seed heads on perennials and grasses that sparkled like jewels in the winter frost but now merely look tired. Suddenly there is a lot to do, and I have a list and a sense of purpose. But first, I think, I might just go and lie with the cats in the catmint and listen to the birds.

SPRING FAVOURITES

Primula veris, or the common cowslip, planted en masse in the kitchen garden at Middleton Lodge in Yorkshire (below), *Helleborus* x *hybridus* 'Double Ellen Red' brings a flush of reddish pink in early spring (opposite above left); *Fritillaria meleagris*, the snake's head fritillary, is an eagerly anticipated arrival (opposite above right); *Narcissus* 'Actaea' grows beautifully in pots and lasts well in water after cutting (opposite below right); *Fritillaria raddeana* grows tall and proud in a pot in sun or shade (opposite below left).

Growing bulbs in pots

BY THE TIME SPRING TRULY ARRIVES IN THE UK, I
AM BESIDE MYSELF WITH IMPATIENCE FOR FLOWERS.
I transfer small pots of bulbs such as muscari, *Iris reticulata* and
Fritillaria michailovskyi into bowls and tall urns and top the earth
with moss to prevent them from drying out. I pop the bowls onto a
bright, cool windowsill and watch as they grow tall and come into
flower, shortening what can feel like a very long winter. After a couple
of weeks, the flowers will grow tall and leggy and collapse into an
exhausted heap. I then snip the flower heads and press them before
replanting the bulbs outside in the moist meadow grass. Not all the
bulbs will thank me for this, and some of them may not flower next
year, but many will. And it cures my longing for spring for a little while.

A SEA OF FLOWERS
Early spring in the kitchen garden
at Middleton Lodge (pages 20–21).

BEAUTIFUL BULBS
Impatient for any kind of colour, in
spring I bring in pots of bulbs that
I gently force into flower in the
warmth of the house. Plant small
spring bulbs like *Iris reticulata* in
pots, keep cool and then plant in
the garden when they've finished
(above). Snowdrops add a delicate
touch to the middle shelf in a tiny
Delft vase, while on the lower shelf
white muscari and the delicate bell-
like flowers of *Fritillaria uva-vulpis*
spill out of their bowls (opposite).

Hellebores are possibly the hardest-working plant in the garden. Where we live, with seasons that seem to be becoming less defined every year, they appear in the borders and pots in late December and can repeat flower all the way through to late May. If you bring potted hellebores inside, put them in a cool, light place and don't let them dry out. They cut really well, but don't snip the flowers as soon as they appear – early hellebore stems are soft and will wilt quickly. Outside, grow hellebores close to a window so that you can enjoy them early on, then when the stamens on the flower have become hardened, you can cut them and they will last in a vase or an arrangement for weeks.

Nothing heralds spring quite like the appearance of narcissus, or daffodils. Big, bold drifts of bright yellow flowers such as *Narcissus* 'February Gold' look impressive planted in the lawn and left to naturalize. I prefer the smaller, paler hybrids for their dainty heads

and paler petals, especially if I'm going to use them individually in an arrangement. Try *Narcissus* 'W. P. Milner' or *N.* 'Actaea' for white petals with a red rim to the trumpet. When cut, narcissus produce a sap that other flowers, such as tulips, take exception to, so I cut them and then leave them on their own for an hour or so before arranging them with other flowers in fresh water. This leads to a longer-lasting collection.

Tulips are possibly my favourite flower to grow in spring, and big, blowsy flowers with striped candy cane markings or in delicate shades of soft butter and pale toffee are at the top of my list. Try 'Charming Lady' for soft apricot flowers that open like peonies, or 'Mount Tacoma' for a creamy white. 'La Belle Epoque' flowers for weeks in tones of palest butterscotch infused with raspberry, while 'Super Parrot' is pure white with a green streak. The onion-shaped bulbs are easy to grow in pots in well-drained soil, and you need very

IN FULL FLOWER
I grow tulips en masse in pots in the garden to cut and bring inside. 'Mount Tacoma' is a creamy white, multi-petalled peony tulip and will last for days in a vase (opposite above).

COAXED INTO BLOOM
Early in spring, I place pots of tiny spring bulbs on a bright windowsill to gently encourage them to flower (above). As long as I don't let them dry out, once they have finished flowering I will plant them out in the garden in the hope that they will flower again the following year.

little space to create a fabulous effect. Tulips will continue to grow in water after you have cut and brought them inside, so form sinuous and graceful lines in an arrangement.

Other spring bulbs that grow well in small pots are *Fritillaria meleagris* or snake's head fritillaries. Small and dainty, they have nodding chequered heads in shades of lilac, mauve and white. These delicate flowers will give movement to any arrangement. I also love *Fritillaria raddeana*. Tall and stately with butter-coloured flowers, it will stand in water in a vase for weeks. Add a few dainty *Fritillaria uva-vulpis* – their thin, wiry stems cut well and look just as good in a glass bottle as they do in a larger arrangement.

FRAGILE BEAUTY
Narcissus 'Chinita', with delicate pale lemon petals that remind me of paper windmills, requires nothing more than a simple glass vase (opposite).

ATTENTION GRABBER
Tulipa 'Apricot Parrot' (above). She's loud and she's a diva, but she mellows beautifully the older she gets and produces some wonderful relaxed shapes when left in a vase for a week or so.

DUTCH STILL LIFE
A 19th-century Delft bough pot is perfect for tulips, and I can't resist tucking in a few more spring delights, including *Narcissus* 'Abba' and *N.* 'Wedding Bell', *Tulipa* 'Bell Song' and a hellebore that has gone to seed and is perfect for cutting.

A CURIOUS MIND

ONE MORNING EARLY IN APRIL I STOOD IN MY STUDIO, HANDS IN MY APRON POCKETS. THE SUN WAS STREAKING THROUGH THE WINDOW, HIGHLIGHTING A FRESHLY SPUN COBWEB IN THE CORNER AND A SMALL POT OF NARCISSUS BULBS THAT STOOD ON A TABLE BEYOND, TALL AND LEGGY, SUFFERING FROM SLIGHT NEGLECT AND LACK OF DIRECT LIGHT.

It was quiet, apart from the sound of Wilson gently snoring under the workbench. The scene was one of tranquillity, yet I felt restless. My mind flickered from one thought to another. Should I plonk some tulips in a vase or arrange them in an urn? Should I leave the studio and spend the morning sending emails? Did I have time to rearrange the collection of dried flowers on the mantelpiece into a thought-provoking vignette?

At the heart of my unease was an opportunity. An opportunity I had only dreamed of, but one that had become a reality and had me wanting to hide with Wilson under the table.

'Are you packed?' asked the husband, poking his head around the door. I nodded.

'Come on,' he said gently. 'What's the worst that can happen?'

'What if I get there and find all my floral abilities have gone, I have nothing to say and they discover that I am, in fact, a total fraud?'

'Just go and enjoy it. Be curious, be yourself and don't take that apron,' said the husband, ushering me out of the door.

'What if I just get lost on the freeway heading out of San Francisco, never to be seen again?' I said, with a last desperate look behind me.

'Then we will come and find you,' he said.

My adventure was to take me to San Francisco to run a workshop with two of my heroes: Gabriela Salazar, with her breathtaking ability to take flowers from the garden and arrange them in a bowl that whispers of utter romance, and Max Gill, who can turn a bowl of flowers into a mini garden. I was star-struck by both of them and their work, and I wasn't sure what I was bringing to the party. I was very ordinary, with a life filled with muddy dogs, cobwebs and an unrelenting passion for gardens and flowers. But that passion had opened up many opportunities, including an invitation to help host this workshop.

The more I allowed myself to observe how people interact with flowers, the more I questioned long-held beliefs that had prevented me from considering a creative life. As a garden designer, for years I had looked at the big picture outside, wondering how I could bring the essence of a garden inside and turn

it into an artwork. My inner voice had kept me safe, turning over and then rejecting my ideas. The creativity that had come so easily to me as a child had been replaced with overthinking and a belief that art was something I should do in my free time as a hobby. By following my instincts and saying yes to opportunities without knowing where they would lead, I found friends who would inspire, places that opened my eyes and a belief that my creativity really was of value.

THE BIGGER PICTURE

I gave one last glance over my shoulder at the daffodils dancing the fandango on a table in the studio and the tulips that needed to be put into water before heading out the door towards a new adventure that would provide me with fresh inspiration (above).

Inspiration

INSPIRATION FOR MY WORK COMES FROM MANY DIFFERENT PLACES. Working in different parts of the world is obviously inspiring (once you've got over the fear of getting on the wrong plane), but there is also inspiration to be found closer to home. A walk in an ancient woodland, for example, the sound of the sea moving across the shore at dusk or shadows cast on a path in the vegetable garden. It can come from a patch of wild sunflowers self-seeded at the roadside, dried magnolia leaves or hand-dyed silks hanging in a studio window to dry.

My work as a garden designer requires me to impose a sense of control on an outdoor space, to devise orderly structures and planting combinations. However, it is often the forgotten tray of potted bulbs left in the gloom of the shed that have grown tall and graceful searching for the light that inspires me the most, along with the bruised blush of leaves on a tree just before they fall or the neglected corner of the garden where much-maligned yet beautiful weeds grow tall in the low afternoon sun.

Eyes bleary from jet lag, I wasn't sure I felt particularly inspired about anything as we got up as early as a lark in the San Francisco morning to gather flowers for our workshop. Max had promised us cuttings from a magnolia tree in his garden, and as we drove over the Bay Bridge to the flower market the dawn broke, throwing pink streaks across the sky that were reflected in the water below and the mirrored glass of the skyscrapers ahead.

The market couldn't fail to inspire – it was spring in a vase. There were tall trolleys of cherry blossom cut that morning, heaps of hellebores piled high on newspapers, buckets of tulips, ranunculus in every delicious colour and early sweet peas.

Max's magnolia provided us with the initial inspiration for our workshop, its delicate chalky white flowers shyly emerging from velvety molten caramel buds. It was lovely enough to pop in a vase all alone, but it would also offer a beautiful sculptural starting point for our work in class.

DELICIOUS MARKET FINDS
Hellebores mingle with butterfly ranunculus and *Fritillaria uva-vulpis* in glass jars ready for workshop guests to enjoy (opposite above left); parrot tulips to tone with my trainers (opposite above right); hellebores all ready to be wrapped (opposite below right); *Ozothamnus diosmifolius*, an Australian native that I could only dream of growing in my British garden, is available from the market (opposite below left).

When choosing your flowers for an arrangement, it is easiest to start with a focal flower that you can't take your eyes off, and then base your further selection around that. The white flowers of the magnolia left the options pretty open, admittedly, but cries of delight could be heard within that vast warehouse of flowers as we filled our arms with flowers in pink, mauve, buttery gold, ochre and palest toffee. After all, it had been a long, hard winter.

Start with a flower that you can't take your eyes off.

FOCAL FLOWER
A precious stem of *Magnolia doltsopa* from Max's garden (opposite above). To go with the magnolia, we piled armfuls of hellebores, *Fritillaria meleagris* 'Alba' and stems of eucalyptus foliage high on the counter. They were a sight for sore eyes (opposite below).

THE FINISHED ARRANGEMENT
Taking the magnolia as her lead, Gabriela pulled together flowering stems of ranunculus in tones of pinks and plum, sweet peas in shades of bruised fig with iridescent bronzed edges that echoed the caramel buds of the magnolia, fritillaries and small stems of spirea into an exquisite bouquet, here enjoying a long drink of water before being wrapped in silk ribbon (above).

A creative muse

WE ALL HAVE A CREATIVE MUSE. Someone somewhere along the line will inspire you to follow a dream that has been hiding in the outer reaches of your brain. Your muse's work will speak to you like a long-lost friend. There is a light-bulb moment, an 'Oh my goodness, that is what I've been thinking but couldn't quite express or form into a cohesive thought!'

Your muse might not be just one person. It could be a whole collection of people and ideas and memories. My work as a garden designer, working on a large scale with trees, anchoring buildings to the landscape and trying to create a 'sense of place', has possibly had the biggest impact on my creative journey. But along the way, different people, objects and places have added to that journey. They have made me question my beliefs and recognize that anything is possible if you have faith in yourself; and that the art of photography is a skill worth pursuing in order to capture the fleeting moments that nature offers.

During my week in San Francisco, Gabriela and Max took my hesitant thoughts on blurring the boundaries between inside and out and gave me the confidence to present them to an audience. Max Gill has worked as a florist for 20 or so years. After college, he followed his dream of becoming an actor until he realized that his passion lay in the garden and with flowers. But those early days, learning about stage sets and considering the role of props and scenery, became

BEAUTIFUL SIMPLICITY
By limiting himself to three ingredients – *Spiraea prunifolia* 'Plena', hellebores and magnolia (above) – Max has created an utterly peaceful composition (opposite).

techniques that he now employs in his arrangements. His graceful lines lead your eye to a focal point and then on a journey through the piece, just as you might 'read' a painting.

Max's garden is his inspiration, and provides him with blossom in spring, clematis in summer and hellebores in winter. As an event florist, he might use the market to source large quantities of roses or peonies, but it is the flowers he grows in his garden and the understanding he has for the way they interact with one other that give his work a painterly quality that makes you wonder if the arrangement is actually growing in the bowl.

finding your voice

WE ALL HAVE OUR OWN UNIQUE VOICE INSIDE. A way of looking at the world, knowing what makes our hearts beat a little faster and how we take our ideas and present them to friends and family as well as potential clients and on social media.

It's a restless, noisy world out there, and it is easy to become distracted by the amount of information that is thrown at us every hour. Lucid thoughts about a creative project tend to hit me at the least opportune moments, like when I'm in the shower and have to use my finger to hastily scribble a few notes in the steam on the glass door to pin down the thought before it flies off to a remote corner of my brain to sit just tantalizingly out of reach.

If you sit around waiting for an inspirational moment to hit you, the chances are you'll be looking at an empty page all day. Explore those things that truly fascinate you rather than whatever is deemed to be the trend of the moment. Look closely at the tiny details right under

SORBET SHADES
Ranunculus in joyful spring colours, from deepest maroon to salmon pink, are wrapped in newspaper to protect their fragile stems (above). With the ends trimmed, they are placed in water overnight to hydrate (opposite). Their multi-petalled blooms will slowly open in the vase. With a bit of care, they will last as a cut flower for 10 days or more. But even a few hours with these beauties would be good enough for me.

your nose. And allow your curiosity and your creativity free rein. Make your own journals (see page 186), press favourite flowers between sheets of cartridge paper inserted within the pages of piles of heavy magazines or invest in a beautiful flower press. Connect with creatives in other fields and draw inspiration from their thoughts and their work to create your own story. Most of all, make a mess experimenting. No one learns to arrange flowers without making some truly questionable arrangements along the way, just as no one becomes a gardener without killing a few plants, however good their intentions might be. Believe me, without a long and sometimes frustrating creative journey, there will be no masterpiece or true sense of satisfaction waiting for you at the end.

CREATIVE ENDEAVOURS

I find inspiration in many different places. Here, I'm captivated by how the subtle shades of pink in the flowers of *Daphne odora* 'Aureomarginata' sit beside the olive tinge of a dried magnolia leaf and several different tones of green paint. I'll record all the details in one of my journals (above).

PRESSING AND PRESERVING

I love to press flowers between the pages of magazines or using a wooden press (above). Place them on a sheet of cartridge paper (or parchment paper) then carefully close the magazine or press and weigh it down. Leave for anything from a couple of days to a few weeks. Flowers are ready once they are dry, but be careful, as they may be brittle. They act as a beautiful reminder of my favourite varieties.

ALL IN THE DETAIL

Take a moment to breathe in the intoxicating scent of *Syringa* 'Maiden's Blush' (above right) or to enjoy the simplicity of a bunch of tulips and daffodils rescued from the garden and popped into a simple glass vase (right).

TRIAL AND ERROR
When it comes to arranging flowers, give yourself time to experiment and learn from your mistakes. Be open to changing your ideas and original intentions. The urn shown opposite finally came together after I spent a couple of days making some truly terrible arrangements and a huge mess in the studio.

BLURRING THE BOUNDARIES

a spring sculpture

NOTHING SIGNIFIES SPRING FOR ME QUITE LIKE THE
HEDGEROWS HERE AT HOME. Early in April, they start to burst
into life with a gentle green haze. The narcissus are in full swing and the
tulips are starting to arrive. Who wouldn't want to bring a bit of that
optimism inside?

Here I've created a spring floral installation, almost a stage set,
inspired by a trip to Italy and time spent sitting on a veranda
overlooking the Tuscan hills. The basic idea can be adapted for use in
any number of different situations – I have used the same principles to
create wedding arches around church doors, freestanding arches in a
field for a summer party and even for an installation at the Chelsea
Flower Show. It might be that there is a fabulous view in your garden
that you want to frame with an arch, then get married underneath, or
alternatively you could create a set like this one
to use as a wonderfully atmospheric backdrop
for wedding (or other celebratory) photographs.
Let your imagination fly free!

FINDING INSPIRATION
Let the atmosphere of a place inspire you to create a moment
of make-believe. The yearning to be back in the rolling hills
near the Tuscan town of Montepulciano that I had visited
a couple of years earlier (right) provided all the inspiration I
needed for this installation (opposite).

You will need

* A large canvas, paint (leftover sample pots are ideal) and paintbrushes, or a photographic or wallpaper wall mural. Photowall have an array of different backdrops (see Sources, pages 204–205).

* Floral snips and wire cutters

* A support for your arch After scratching my head about how to fix wires into old church walls (you can't), I created a freestanding support that dismantles for easy transport. I made this from a paving stone with an umbrella parasol screwed into it, which holds a tall hazel pole. A flat, square garden umbrella stand and a broom handle would work equally well.

* Grave vases These are plastic containers used to hold water and flowers on a grave. They come in a variety of different sizes and can be reused.

* Bindwire

* Small nail and hammer

* Chicken wire

* Decorative moss

* Florist's or other bucket to hold water at the base

* A small watering can

* A stepladder

* Orchid vials or water tubes with spiked ends to hold short stems

Flowers and stems

* Structural branches x 3 or 4 (as long as possible). I am using *Salix caprea* (goat willow), with its yellow catkins, and amelanchier.

* Filler flowers x 2 bucketfuls. I'm using *Prunus spinosa* (blackthorn) in flower and *Spiraea japonica* 'Goldflame'.

* Focal flowers x 15. For a natural look, use whatever is in season in the garden. I'm using *Tulipa* 'La Belle Epoque', *Narcissus* 'Chinita' and *N.* 'Thalia'.

* Gestural moments x 10. These long, wispy stems will give your installation a naturalistic feel. I'm using privet, *Spiraea* 'Arguta' (bridal wreath), *Clematis vitalba* (old man's beard) and wild honeysuckle.

Step 1

Allow your creativity free rein and use your paints to create an atmospheric mural backdrop, as I have done here. Alternatively, use a photographic or wallpaper mural to set your scene.

Step 2

Cut and condition your flowers. Try and do this very early the morning before you make the installation and leave the blooms in a cool, dark place to have a good long drink overnight.

*I was inspired by the
Tusan landscape.*

the rim of the tube and attach it to a small nail banged into the pole. With the tube held in place, I wrap a square of chicken wire around it, fasten it in place with bindwire and backfill with moss to conceal the plastic.

step 5

When all the grave vases are attached, push the pole into your base (if you are outside, you might want to anchor it further with a sandbag). On the base, I stand a florist's bucket full of water. Start to insert long, structural branches. Hold longer ones in place by wiring them to the support with a length of bindwire. Look for branches with a natural curve at the top that will form an arched shape.

step 3

Create the structural backbone of your installation. As explained on page 46, I have made a pole and base that travels with me and can be adapted for each event. The same effect can be created using a garden umbrella base and a broom handle or wooden pole.

step 4

As well as a support, your flowers will need water. I fasten small plastic grave vases at regular intervals along the hazel pole. To do this, wind bindwire around

step 7

Carry on inserting the filler flowers to cram the bucket with plenty of foliage and blossom. Your installation needs to look as if it is part of the landscape, not as if it has landed from outer space.

step 8

As you work your way up the support, you may find some stems aren't long enough to reach the grave vases. In this case, I use orchid vials or water tubes with spikes on the bottom. Fill them with water, insert a stem, then push them into the moss-covered chicken wire wherever desired.

step 6

Fill all the grave vases with water, using a small watering can. If the installation is likely to be outside for a while, you may need to top these up during the event, as the flowers will drink a lot of water, especially if it's windy or hot.

step 10

Add a few dried vine tendrils if you have them, or have a forage to see what's left in the garden or hedgerows after the winter. I have placed a handful of *Clematis vitalba* around the base to draw the eye away from the florist's bucket. And there you have it – an Italian landscape to lose yourself in for a while. Let me just go and find myself a chair...

step 9

'La Belle Epoque' tulips are quite big and blowsy. I place them in clusters of 3 or 5 at the base of the installation, with a few other scattered stems of narcissus working their way skyward. I feel it looks more effortless and natural if the heavier blooms are at the base and the more delicate stems are closer to the top, as if searching for the sun.

An Italian landscape to lose yourself in.

EARLY SUMMER

a season of

timeless romance

'It was June, and the world smelled of roses.
The sunshine was like powdered gold
over the grassy hillside.'

MAUD HART LOVELACE, *Betsy-Tacy and Tib*

CONNECTING TO THE LANDSCAPE

THE GARDEN IS FULL OF PROMISE AND ENTHUSIASM IN EARLY SUMMER, BUT WITHOUT THE BRASH AUDACITY OF SPRING.

The roses and poppies are bursting with buds, while wild carrot and other self-seeded umbellifers line the hedgerows in a cloud of froth. Foliage that is still fresh and green from the spring rain uncurls in the sun, and the nightingale sings. By the time late summer arrives, the landscape will have turned a shade of parchment. The roses will have had their moment, eclipsed by the arrival of late summer blooms in antique jewel tones. So early summer takes her opportunity. Kicking off her shoes, she readies herself with quiet grace and elegance, gathering all her thoughts and energy, planning her best garden party ever.

MIDSUMMER MEADOW
A simple mown path cuts through a midsummer meadow of ox-eye daisies and curves out of sight, inviting you to explore a garden that blends effortlessly with the countryside beyond (opposite). The roses reach their peak at this time of year, and the luscious climber 'The Generous Gardener' is a particular favourite (right).

The Garden

ON MY WAY TO THE GREENHOUSE, I BREATHE IN
THE SUMMER GARDEN SMELLS OF FRESHLY MOWN
GRASS AND LILAC. I need to do some seed sowing and wrestle my
dahlia tubers out of the pots they were started in before planting them
out in the raised beds. There are howls of rage from the lawn as Wilson
runs off with a croquet ball that was being thwacked between hoops
by the husband and teenager, and I discover that my strawberries have
been eaten by the squirrel family who live at the bottom of the garden.
They sit in the trees and drop the green stalks on the Welsh Whippet's
head, while he wonders whether the cat can teach him to climb trees.

EASY COMPANIONS
The small plum flowers of
Sanguisorba 'Tanna' flower from
early June, and here are happily
sharing space with slightly later
flowering white penstemons and
Thalictrum delavayi, which keep on
going until late September (above).

HAPPILY DRIFTING
The old brick walls that surround
the kitchen garden at Middleton
Lodge in Yorkshire radiate heat
drawn from the summer sun back
into the garden, and provide a
wonderful backdrop to drifts of
salvias, astrantias, geraniums and
euphorbias (opposite).

HIGH SUMMER SHADES
Wafting in the breeze, the pincushion flowers
of *Knautia macedonica* 'Melton Pastels' come in
pastel shades of pinks, blues and purple. These
soft colours epitomize the early summer garden.

FLOWERS IN THE SKY

NOT EVERYONE HAS THE LUXURY OF A GARDEN. If you live in an apartment, balcony gardening can be a brilliant way to create an outside space filled with pots. And if you happen to have a rooftop, then why not garden in the sky? I was hugely inspired by a visit to Bluma Farm, run by Joanna Letz in Berkeley, California. The garden was purpose-built above college accommodation for students, and is about a quarter hectare/half an acre in total. The beds are filled with a special type of enriched organic soil that is lightweight enough not to cause structural problems to the building and drains freely. The beds are irrigated daily from rainwater harvesting tanks, and during the planting season Joanna uses a liquid fertilizer, fed through the irrigation system, that is 100% organic fish emulsion.

Stepping out of the lift onto the rooftop is an experience like nothing else – thanks to the height of the building, you are far removed from the noise of traffic and daily life below. Gabriela and I visited in June, when there were sweet peas, zinnias, chocolate cosmos and penstemons jostling for space in the beds. While Gabby chose flowers for our workshop guests, I wandered around and wondered if the husband would mind if I became Joanna's full-time assistant and slept

SKY HIGH
Joanna Letz surveys her rooftop garden, surrounded by a white froth of *Eriogonum giganteum* (St Catherine's Lace), blue salvias and *Lagurus ovatus* (above and opposite). Joanna has learned through trial and error which plants love it up in the sky, and which don't. Spring bulbs don't do very well, for example, but lavender thrives.

in the shed, while scanning the university website to see if I could sign up as a student and claim a rooftop bedroom there and then. I was happy to consider anything – never had Biophysics looked so appealing.

GROWING FLOWERS
to bring inside

I'VE ALWAYS DRAGGED NATURE INSIDE. AT UNIVERSITY, I PLANTED
UP A WIRE BASKET WITH TRAILING VERBENAS AND PANSIES AND
HUNG IT OFF A WARDROBE IN MY SHARED STUDENT BEDROOM.

Then there was the breathtakingly sculptural wind-blown branch found at the side of the road that I just couldn't leave behind. I convinced the husband it would be easy to fit into our small car if he only pulled the driver's seat a little further forward. He drove home with his nose squashed against the windscreen, muttering crossly and refusing point-blank to see the qualities of the branch I fawned over.

By the time I had a garden of my own, I was reluctant to cut flowers that I had spent so long growing. My design for rivers of perennial grasses leading the eye towards an open vista in the garden looked so good, with tall heleniums and roses enjoying the afternoon sun, that I couldn't bring myself to cut anything. But eventually my desire to create floral arrangements drove me to consider the options that would work best for me.

I knew I didn't need a cutting garden to provide me with buckets of blooms for a wedding or event. I have my friend Carol for that. She can provide 30 buckets of seasonal flowers without turning a hair. You need skill, knowledge and patience to grow rows and rows of shrubs, perennials and annuals to the standard required by florists for weddings and events. It is a full-time job and one you must be passionate about.

I just wanted to grow my favourite flowers. They would fill our raised beds with colour and joy through the growing season, and also give me a chance to experiment with arrangements and fill the house with colour and scent. Believe me, you don't need a huge amount of space to grow flowers to cut – some of the most beautiful and creative flower-filled spaces I've seen have been tiny balcony and roof gardens.

SUMMER ABUNDANCE
You don't need to grow armfuls of flowers to enjoy them inside. Lupins, verbascums and pale yellow *Aquilegia chrysantha* will all grow in a container. Coriander has delicate white flowers if allowed to bolt and will live on a windowsill. (opposite).

Growing in pots

OUR GARDEN WAS DESIGNED TO PROVIDE SOMEWHERE TO SIT CLOSE TO THE KITCHEN DOORS during the warmer months. Here, I grow herbs in pots – lavender, thyme, oregano and mint. We cook with them, and I like to leave them to flower in late summer and then form small sculptures in the winter frost and snow.

In summer, my pots are filled with hardy annuals and perennials that I cut and bring inside. I grow *Phlox drummondii* with evocative names such as 'Crème Brûlée' and 'Cherry Caramel' from seed. They take up little space but really earn their keep, with caramel-coloured flowers from late May right through to the first frosts, if you keep cutting them. I also grow calendulas in shades of cantaloupe, including a variety called 'Pink Surprise', which in my experience really isn't very pink at all. Maybe that's the surprise?

Agrostemma githago (the common corncockle) used to be found in cornfields but is now quite rare due to overuse of herbicides. Grow it in pots or raised beds alongside blue and pink cornflowers for flowers that cut and last well in water and remind you of cornfields of times past.

And then there are sweet peas, or *Lathyrus odoratus*. I grow these in vintage dolly tubs by the back door for their wonderful scent, and in raised beds with the runner beans in the garden. Peas like to develop a long root and dislike being disturbed once they have been planted, so I start mine in late winter or early spring using seeds from a specialist grower. I soak the seeds on a damp cloth and leave them in a plastic bag for a week or so. When they start to shoot, I plant them in root trainers that open sideways to avoid root disturbance when planted out, or in cardboard toilet roll inners that can be planted with the seedling and will biodegrade as the root grows.

When the pea shoots are about 2.5cm/1in tall, I move them into the cool greenhouse with plenty of direct light – they grow too tall and leggy in the warmth of the house. Once the danger of late frosts has passed, I plant them out. They need plenty of water and are greedy for food. Put lots of well-rotted horse or chicken manure in the base of the pot or planting

OTHER BEAUTIES TO GROW IN POTS
FOR CUTTING:

Achillea These are brilliant filler flowers for bowls and bouquets alike.

Sedum Wonderful in the late summer garden in tones of deep plum through to crushed raspberry. I plant sedum in drifts within the herbaceous bed, but also have short ones in pots dotted around the courtyard. They work well for softening the front of a bowl or urn arrangement.

Rudbeckia There are many different varieties of rudbeckia that work well in the garden if you have well-drained soil and a sunny aspect. *Rudbeckia hirta* 'Sahara', in tones of toffee, honeycomb and vintage rose, will give you a brilliant abundance of flowers later in summer. They are easily grown from seed.

Aquilegia Once planted, these cottage garden classics will happily self-seed all over your garden.

trench and build them a support from hazel sticks that they can climb up. They will reward you with oodles of flowers that you must cut frequently, or they will put their energy into making seeds rather than flowers.

Poppies remind me of my childhood, as my grandmother used to plant big scarlet oriental ones in her garden. I love them, but they take up a lot of room in the flowerbed and can be a one-minute wonder in our wet Welsh weather. Instead, I sow annual Shirley and California poppies from seed, both of which are easy to grow. There are some truly breathtaking varieties that I urge you to try. *Papaver rhoeas* 'Amazing Grey' is a haunting lilac grey that reminds me of Parma violet sweets. It's quietly determined and defies the wet and cold weather here in North Wales to flower on regardless until the first frosts. It prefers to be outside really, but if cut for indoors it will last two or three days in water if you first sear the stems in boiling water. Poppies are a fleeting moment, but oh what a moment!

Wild strawberries You might need to net these if you have squirrels, as half-eaten green stalks don't strike quite the right note in an arrangement.

Blueberries The birds and the teenager like these, and they grow happily in a pot near the house planted in the acidic soil they prefer.

Nasturtium I steer clear of the bright orange ones, and plant ones with interesting names such as 'Ladybird Rose' and 'Tip Top Apricot'.

Tomato Red Currant I fight a losing battle with these, as it would appear there isn't anyone who doesn't like to pop a tiny tomato in their mouth. So I plant lots everywhere: in pots by the back door, in the greenhouse and in the raised beds. The seeds are so tiny that I usually end up with a few random self-seeded ones, so at least I have a few to add to late summer arrangements.

Growing in raised beds

THERE ARE A FEW THINGS THAT JUST DON'T GROW WELL IN POTS. As hard as I water and feed, they sulk and take on a look of misery. When this is the case, it's best not to try and fight nature. Don't drive yourself demented trying to grow plants that don't like your soil or aspect. There are other possibilities out there that will work for you.

I adore roses. Big, old-fashioned roses in muted colours on long stems with an exquisite scent. I use them a lot in my arrangements, as focal flowers or in relaxed clusters around the edges, with petals tumbling on the table just as they might in the garden.

My roses grow happily in raised beds, which we constructed from reclaimed timber found discarded in the garden undergrowth when we moved in. As we are on the side of a mountain, our soil is sandy and filled with large stones. Long gone are the days when I could encourage my toddler son to fill buckets with stones from the soil in return for an ice lolly, and the husband was never quite so easily bribed. So we built up and filled the raised beds with compost from the garden plus topsoil. They are easier to maintain, kinder to my back and give the roses plenty of depth for their roots.

FLOWERS TO SWOON OVER
Combine late-flowering peony tulips with early flowering poppies, larkspur and roses for delicious colour combinations as spring merges into summer (opposite above). As the summer months pass, flower colours go from pastel to jewel-like, with topaz *Rudbeckia hirta* 'Sahara' and deep plummy pink sedums flowering into autumn (opposite above and below).

My favourite roses

MY FAVOURITE ROSE
'Julia's Rose': utterly exquisite tones of fawn and parchment with occasional flushes of raspberry. My 'couldn't be without' garden rose (above).

YOU CAN LOSE YOURSELF FOR DAYS – MONTHS EVEN – CHOOSING ROSES FOR CUTTING. Immerse yourself in rose catalogues and visit gardens and flower shows for inspiration. Over time, I have learned which roses grow best for me and which I prefer to work with. Grow those you love and don't be afraid to experiment, but do understand your soil. There are roses for all conditions, and they will amply reward you for getting it right.

'Westerland' A tall early climber with large, high-voltage apricot open flowers that put on a second and third repeat bloom. However, it has thorns the size of small machetes, and after a few seasons working with arms that looked as if I'd had a fight with a barbed-wire fence, 'Westerland' now grows over a rose arch in the garden. We respect each other from a distance.

'Julia's Rose' A firm favourite in the muted parchment tones I favour. 'Julia' is delicate, with thin stems, and needs lots of encouragement on a daily basis, but once she flowers, she is resolute. Just a handful of flowers once in the season makes it all worthwhile.

'Champagne Moment' This creamy white beauty with a pale apricot centre flowers abundantly throughout the season. I don't prune it hard in winter, instead leaving long stems that I can cut and drape over the edges of urns to give a relaxed and unassuming air in summer and autumn arrangements.

'Koko Loko' A dusty pink rose exuding pure romance. Assertive but not aggressive, 'Koko' works well as a focal flower and is a firm favourite with both gardeners and florists alike.

'The Lark Ascending' There is a steely determination and persistence to this graceful golden-apricot rose. It flowers all season long with open cups that speak of vulnerability yet have an undeniable strength. 'Lark' lasts for a least a week in water and slowly decays in an utterly heartbreaking but romantic way.

'Desdemona' The earliest white rose to flower in mid-May, with a generous second flush in August. She is deliciously scented and lasts well in water, making it excellent for bridal work.

OTHER FLOWERS AND FOLIAGE THAT ARE EASY TO GROW IN POTS OR BEDS:

Scabious Little flowers like pincushions carried on tall, wiry stems in colours of deep wine, strawberry pink and sky blue.

Geums Early flowering gems in shades of tangerine and palest pinks with slightly ruffled petals.

Wild carrot (*Daucus carota* 'Dara') The perfect umbellifer, this self-seeds from one year to the next and looks very happy simply popped in a glass vase.

Dahlias These are easy to grow in raised beds, pots and the ground. They enjoy moist but well-drained soil and lots of sun. I grow them for late summer colour when the roses are waning – just as the garden feels a bit tired and dry, the dahlias are getting into their stride. Available in a huge range of colours, and with flower

heads the size of dinner plates, it's worth studying the descriptions of the flower sizes before you buy your tubers. These will arrive in late winter. Keep them dry until you are ready to plant them in the garden, or start them off in pots with compost in a greenhouse and plant them out once all danger of frost has passed.

Foliage I don't fill my arrangements with masses of green or foliage, and I usually take most of the leaves off a flowering stem such as rose or late summer *Leycesteria formosa.* Green can flatten and dominate an arrangement, and I would rather the focus was on the flower. However, there are certain shrubs and trees that I grow, including the following.

Amelanchier canadensis I love this tree for its open habit and good looks all year round. Very delicate white flowers in spring are followed by coppery bronzed leaves in autumn. The perfect tree for a small garden. Amelanchier alnifolia 'Obelisk' can even be grown in a pot on the terrace.

FLOWERS FOR RAISED BEDS
Helichrysum bracteatum 'Salmon Rose' is a summer beauty to cut and dry to use later in the year (above).
Geum 'Cosmopolitan' (Cocktails Series) has apricot and pink frilly petals that become paler with age (left).

Rosa 'Koko Loco' in her dusky pink skirts is the focal point flower in a 19th-century urn arrangement (left and opposite). For me, the flowers of early summer are the epitome of timeless romance. Here, pale *Rosa* 'Champagne Moment' tumbles over the right-hand side of the urn with the foliage of *Rosa glauca* tucked underneath, while sweet peas scramble upwards. The pale calendulas and *Phlox drummondii* 'Crème Brûlée' placed along the front connect and balance the colours from left to right.

Prunus 'Accolade' I'm not really a pink fan, but there is something about the ornamental cherry in mid-March that makes my heart sing. A single branch covered in pink blossom in a small vase can be all you need to brighten your day.

Spiraea 'Arguta' (bridal wreath) Spring is all about froth, blossom and confetti in the air, and this spirea is no exception. Early to flower, it has long, arching sprays of tiny white flowers and fresh green leaves that bring arrangements an exuberant yet light touch.

Hydrangea paniculata 'Limelight' This really hits its stride in late summer and into autumn. I love it in the border, catching the late summer sun. It adds a light touch to any arrangement and also dries beautifully.

Cotinus 'Grace' Cotinus, or smoke bush, is a gift in late summer, with hazy flower plumes giving the impression of puffs of smoke. Strip the leaves and just use the 'smoke', or wait until the leaves turn delicious shades of orange and red in autumn.

Look out for other attractive foliage late in summer. As autumn approaches, many shrubs and small trees will turn beautiful shades of fig and plum – *Thalictrum* 'Black Stockings' is a perfect case in point.

THE HEIGHT OF SUMMER

A low vintage soup bowl full of tumbling summer roses, annual phlox, chives and currant tomato vines benefits from a plinth made from old books (above). Not only do the books gently reflect the pink tones, but it is also very helpful in lifting the bowl higher off the table, meaning you don't need to bend down too far to breathe in the wonderful summer scents.

A FLOWERY WELCOME

My porch at home often becomes a place to condition the flowers I've brought home or cut from the garden, and they seem more than happy to share the space with baskets of shoes and hanging coats and hats (opposite). I leave them to have a long drink of water and relax in the gentle warmth for at least 12 hours, which makes them easy to work with.

FLOWERS FOR ENTERTAINING

a summer table

COME EARLY SUMMER, THE GARDEN WILL BE FULL OF FLOWERS AND FOLIAGE THAT I CAN GATHER IN ARMFULS AND BRING INSIDE. I will use them to create bowls of flowers on a table that friends and family can crowd around all together. The room is filled with the heady scents of roses, herbs, sweet peas and strawberries that I have saved from the clutches of the squirrels at the bottom of the garden. But you really don't need a celebration or event as an excuse to bring the outside in any time of the year. Any flowers popped in a vase or jar are a joy and will add colour and effortless beauty to your home. And if you don't have a garden, why not grow a pot of mint or a scented pelargonium on a sunny windowsill and gently rub the leaves every time you pass them for a wonderful release of scent.

READY FOR THE FEAST
Dress your room and set your table with low bowls of flowers filled with roses, herbs, lavenders and *Delphinium consolida* in the richest blue. Trailing vines wrap around tall, elegant candlesticks and long, sculptural branches that fill the space with fresh green leaves (left).

looks lovely. There will always be something you can be creative with, whatever the time of year. However, to give you a rough idea, for this arrangement I would suggest the following:

✳ **Structural branches or long vines x 2 or 3.** Try *Exochorda racemosa*, *Akebia quinata* (chocolate vine) or *Rosa glauca* foliage. These will give your arrangement form and shape.

✳ **Focal flowers x 5.** I'm using roses, but rudbeckias or dahlias would also work well.

✳ **Filler Flowers x 3.** Try hellebores and clematis.

✳ **Gestural moments x 5**, such as thin stems of *Consolida ajacis* (larkspur), verbascum, *Papaver nudicaule* (Icelandic poppy) or sweet peas.

✳ **Textural elements x 4.** Dried helichrysum (strawflower) or dried hydrangea, *Clematis vitalba* (old man's beard), or coriander/ cilantro or marjoram that has gone to flower – anything that will add fluff and give your arrangement softness.

You will need

✳ Several small bowls of a similar size

✳ Chicken wire and floral tape

flowers and stems

I don't stem count or make precise recipes for the number of flowers I need in an arrangement. Instead, I go into the garden on the morning of a party and pick whatever

step 1

For my table centrepieces, I'm using simple white bowls with a gently flared rim that will allow the flowers to relax over the sides. The bowls measure about 10 x 10cm/4 x 4in. Anything bigger will need large quantities of flowers to fill, and anything tall and tapered will become unstable once filled with water and heavy blooms. To support the flowers in the bowl, I'm using a small roll of chicken wire held in place with floral tape. If you can see the tape once you've finished, gently pull it away from the rim and tuck it under the flowers.

step 2

I start by creating the basic structural elements, in this case formed from a few stems of *Exochorda racemosa*. *Rosa glauca* would also work well, and I sometimes use sprigs of *Carpinus betulus* in the autumn, when its leaves are turning golden brown.

I go into the garden and pick whatever looks lovely.

step 3

Choose your flowers. I'm using the first of the roses as my focal point. Try *Rosa* 'English Miss', 'A Shropshire Lad' and 'Margaret Merril' for a soft summer palette of blush pinks and creamy whites.

step 4

Cut the rose stems short and push them into the chicken wire framework. Don't cut all the stems to exactly the same length, but stagger them slightly so that the roses don't look too uniform in the bowl. I am deliberately keeping the arrangement quite low, as I am going to position the bowls down the centre of the table like a table runner.

step 5

Once the roses are in place, I add longer stems such as a white clematis, *Consolida ajacis* (larkspur) and a couple of hellebores that have turned a wonderful muted purple with age.

step 6

These arrangements will be seen in the round, so turn your bowl around and look at it from every angle. Add textural elements, such as the helichrysum and the delicate multi-petalled hydrangea head last, so that they almost seem to float above the other flowers.

step 7

Lay the table and place your bowls
of flowers at regular intervals down
the centre. Connect them using long,
loose strands of clematis, or whatever
trailing vine you are using. Light
candles in holders and mix old and
new tableware. Now pour yourself
a glass of something bubbly or a
well-earned cup of tea. Enjoy! Bowls
of flowers like these should last for a
couple of days, depending on the heat
of the room. Don't forget to top them
up with water if they need it.

*Any flowers
popped in a vase or
jar are a joy.*

LATE SUMMER

a season of slow living

'I believe the nicest and sweetest days are not
those on which anything very splendid
or wonderful or exciting happens but just
those that bring simple little pleasures,
following one another softly...'

L.M. MONTGOMERY, *Anne of Green Gables*

CONNECTING TO THE LANDSCAPE

THE LAZY, HAZY DAYS OF LATE SUMMER BEFORE THE CHILDREN GO BACK TO SCHOOL FILL ME WITH NOSTALGIA FOR LONG, HOT AFTERNOONS SPENT PICNICKING ON AN OLD BLANKET UNDER THE SHADE OF AN ANCIENT OAK TREE WITH FAR-REACHING VIEWS OF THE COUNTRYSIDE.

I have a moment of desire to join the throngs of visitors to all the open gardens up and down the land that are currently filled with a riot of sensuous colour and flowers jostling for their moment in the golden summer light. But another part of me is content with just lying where I am, embracing the lethargy that only comes with afternoons like these.

Eventually my constant yearning for colour inspiration and exciting new planting discoveries that will inform my work for the months ahead lures me away from the deep shade of the oak tree. I make a plan to dig out my camera and find a few hours at sunrise to capture some of the utterly peaceful moments of high summer.

ABOUT SUNRISE
In buttermilk shades, the annual helianthus reaches her face towards the early morning sun just starting to rise above the walled garden at Broadfield Court in Herefordshire (opposite).

The Garden

THE ENERGY OF THE EARLY SUMMER
GARDEN HAS SLOWED. The fields of wheat all
around us have turned the colour of gold and there is
a flurry of combine harvesters snaking up and down,
leaving acres of yellow stubble behind them.

Most of my garden seems to be in my studio. Or at
least those were the husband's observations the other
day, as I attempted to make my way past bundles of
hanging flowers at various stages of drying, buckets
of freshly picked dahlias for arrangements and a large
wooden stepladder, its steps scattered with glass jars
filled with paintbrushes or pigments for the blank
canvas that is stretched across one wall.

The studio doors are open and a soft breeze flutters
a pile of paperwork that's waiting to be dealt with.
But not today. Today the sun is breaking through the
clouds and filling the studio with light. I want to be
outside, enjoying the warmth of the sun on my arms.

I take a trowel and trug, intending to weed a bed
under the trees. But I've forgotten my gloves and the
50 yards back to the house to get them seems too
far, so I sit awhile in the dappled shade under the
trees and watch an escapee chicken who, with some
determination, is making her way across the vegetable
patch to the ripe tomatoes.

The cutting beds need attention. The dahlias are
just coming into their own and the stakes are groaning
beneath their weight. The roses have had their second
flush and are starting to slow down. I adore them all
the more for it. They take on a soft, easy and utterly
romantic elegance, as if they are now more comfortable
in their petals. The colours are muted and the scent is
intoxicating. I pause and breathe this all in.

LATE SUMMER DAYS

Mornings are filled with taking inspiration from the gardens at Broadfield Court (above left) and marvelling at majestic white *Cleome hassleriana* basking in the sun at the back of a free-draining border, while back at home Wilson is impatient for an afternoon walk through fields of ripening corn (above right). Newly baled hay dots the fields, ready to feed cattle during the winter (right).

SLOW LIVING

SLOW LIVING MEANS SOMETHING DIFFERENT FOR ALL OF US. FOR ME, IT IS ABOUT TAKING STOCK OF ALL THE INFORMATION AND MATERIALISM THAT IS THROWN IN OUR DIRECTION ON AN HOURLY BASIS AND CHOOSING WHAT, FROM THAT, MAKES ME REALLY HAPPY AND TRULY DESERVES MY ATTENTION.

In the late summer, before the bare-root season begins in November and I need to step things up in the garden, I give myself permission just to sit for a while in the long grass with the Whippet. At this time of year, seed and bulb catalogues start to pop through the letter box on an hourly basis, and before I pore over them and order a thousand bulbs to make the garden look even better next year, I try to absorb all the experiences that it has given me this year. Often we are in such a hurry, hunting for newer and better experiences, that we forget to pause and remember the wonderful ones we have already had.

These wonderful moments are often fleeting, like sticking your head out of the window on a clear and frosty night and watching the stars. Or there's the comedy run and excited clucking that your one and only five-year-old chicken makes when you feed her kale leaves. It could be re-reading a book that you loved for the third time in a row, just because. Or the long hug from the teenager who left home for a new job just before the world went into lockdown and who you've missed every minute since. It's reliving that lovely, simple family holiday you took as a child when you all piled into a car that was more or less tied together with string and drove halfway across Europe. Or having an unexpected free hour to wander around your friend's walled garden, in which she's tirelessly creating her very own version of heaven. It could be the rose bush that is having a third glorious hurrah, despite the wettest summer in years, or the nasturtium that you thought had done her thing for this year but is now full of exuberance and joy…it's the seed catalogue!

LATE SUMMER ABUNDANCE
Lush beauties of the summer garden. A hazy cloud of *Dianthus carthusianorum* in Carol's summer garden (opposite above left); *Cirsium arvense* (creeping thistle) reaches for the sky in the hedgerows (opposite above right); the delicate, star-shaped flowers of *Gaura lindheimeri* 'Whirling Butterflies' (opposite below right); *Centaurea cyanus* 'Blue Ball' leans towards the sun in the raised beds at home (opposite below left);

Carol's Garden

OUR GARDEN IS MOSTLY LAID TO LAWN AND HEDGING. I had grand plans for it when we bought our rambling ruin eight years ago. Having designed gardens for others for 20 years, I yearned for a garden all for myself. I wanted deep flower beds, vines and shrubs, a greenhouse and a shed. Most of all, I wanted it all to look perfect.

But reality soon kicked in. I couldn't possibly maintain deep beds, or afford the time and money they require. I really needed to ask myself the questions that I always ask new clients: exactly how much time do you want to spend gardening?

I wanted to be able to enjoy the time I had in the garden rather than to resent it. My garden had become a place that needed to sparkle for others instead of providing me with a way to slow down and connect to nature. So I reduced the size of the planting and kept it all in one place between the kitchen and studio doors, with big chairs on a hardwood deck placed to catch the late morning and afternoon sun, and laid the rest to lawn, compost and mud holes for the dogs.

I have a small cutting garden full of roses, rudbeckias, dahlias, sweet peas, amaranthus, annual phlox and scabious. Here, I grow achilleas in pots,

as well as geraniums, penstemons, sedums and herbs. There are tulips and narcissus in spring, small tomatoes in summer, chrysanthemums for autumn and viburnum, amelanchier, stewartias, cotinus and acers for year-round seasonal interest. And when I need large quantities of flowers for an event, I go to my friend Carol and her flower farm.

Carol grows on approximately a third of a hectare/ an acre in Cheshire, about an hour's drive away, and I visit her whenever I get the opportunity. Carol is no fuss, has scant regard for the latest fashionable bloom that demands endless attention and refuses to grow flowers that can't survive in the local conditions or alongside each other. She will show you with pride her trays of seedlings, cosseted under a heat light in early spring. Every inch of soil is used, so each plant must earn its keep. Any sign of a less than positive outlook and it's out. The same goes for the florists who clamour for her cut flowers during the growing season. Carol wants to know that they are going to really love her flowers and not do unspeakable things to them, like stick them in floral foam. Her flowers are her children, and the result is sublime.

A RIVER OF PINK
A river of *Echinacea purpurea* growing in Carol's garden (opposite). Planted en masse like this, they make a bold statement and look wonderful with late summer grasses for a prairie feel. Alternatively, grow a few in free-draining pots in the sun for cutting.

HIGH SUMMER BORDERS
Early morning sun filters through the gaggle
of tall annual cosmos and dahlias in the walled
garden at Broadfield Court, while the zinnias in
front await their moment in the sunlight.

BRINGING THE OUTSIDE IN

I'M NOT SURE CAROL WOULD AGREE THAT HER LIFE IS THE EPITOME OF SLOW LIVING. FLOWER FARMING IS HARD PHYSICAL WORK IN ALL SEASONS AND ALL WEATHERS.

RELIABLE ROSES
Rosa 'Julia's Rose' and a single 'Café Latte' enjoy a long drink of water in the studio (opposite), while 'The Lark Ascending' repeat flowers right through the summer (above).

I know from the years I have spent designing and planting gardens that at the end of some days I can hardly even bend to take off my boots. But there is something about feeling the soil between your fingers, smelling the rich, crumbling compost that you know is going to feed and nourish your plants and watching tiny, tiny seeds that you sowed sprout in the greenhouse and the tomatoes ripen in the sun that keeps me curious and full of hope.

I garden at home because it quietens my mind. It stops me thinking about me as I watch the blackbirds eat the crab apples hanging off the tree in the late afternoon sun, or the birds stamping on the lawn after the rain doing a worm dance. It also makes me pause, take stock and find inspiration. When I get to the point where my knees ache to bend, I might go over to Carol's. I'm given a mug of tea and I wander. Sometimes I take a bucket to snip blooms to arrange when I get home, just for me, flowers that I don't grow in my garden. Sometimes I will pick for a wedding. Occasionally, I do both.

I stand for a moment within the mass of dahlias sunning themselves in the rays of the low afternoon sun. I snip a few exquisite roses in deep sumptuous magenta and others the colour of bruised, ripened figs. They will work in an urn arrangement, or possibly I'll leave them in a simple glass vase. They need no further adornment. *Rosa* 'The Lark Ascending' has opened up on her long, arching stems. She looks relaxed and happy, and I can use her in a bowl. 'Julia's Rose' is having her glorious, unassuming moment and there are a number of stems to cut. I let out a little whoop. I now have an armful of the softest butterscotch roses to turn into a bouquet that will make a bride very happy at the weekend. I cut the stems as long as I can without disturbing new shoots forming lower down. The roses

Before I know it, my wander has turned into a van full of buckets filled with colour and scent. I pay my dues and make my way home to unload my treasure, re-cut the stems on an angle with my sharp florist snips and plunge the flowers into deep, cool water. I leave them in the cold studio overnight. By morning they are revived, faces turned towards the light, all ready and waiting to be arranged.

And me? Those moments in which I have given myself permission to just breathe deeply have recharged and revived my creative being. For a moment I have stopped thinking about the impossible and the tricky. I'm focused on what is right here, looking simply perfect, under my nose right now, and I am excited for the day ahead.

will need a long drink in my cool studio before their big day, and, lucky me, I get to enjoy them all to myself for a little while.

I spy pale pink *Hydrangea arborescens* 'Invincibelle Spirit' growing under the shade of the hanging tree canopy. So delicate. I cut a couple of long stems. I would love to use them in the bride's bouquet, but they will wilt before she gets to the end of the aisle, and if any earwigs still snoozing in the dahlia petals tumble out onto the bride's dress as she whispers 'I do', I'll be the least popular florist in town. The hydrangea can keep me company instead. Later on, in autumn, I will cut more of these and they will last and then dry or press beautifully.

FLOWERS TO SWOON OVER

Dahlia 'Preference' is laid out on the studio bench before being selected to include in an urn arrangement (opposite above). Buckets of *Echinacea purpurea* 'Green Twister', scabious, zinnias, rudbeckias and achilleas nestle in buckets of water and jars in a shady spot inside (opposite below). Cut your flowers from the garden in the early morning or early evening when the heat of the day is fading and leave them to drink in water overnight, like these stems of *Hydrangea arborescens* 'Invincibelle Spirit' (right). They will last far longer in an arrangement or bouquet if they have had time to fully hydrate.

ELEGANTLY SLUMPING

As the energy in the garden slows, my arrangements take on an elegant slump (left). This one combines *Rosa* 'Gentle Hermione' with *Dahlia* 'Wizard of Oz', *Echinacea pallida*, some flowering purple basil that smells delicious, thalictrum leaves and *Spiraea* 'Arguta' (bridal wreath) foliage cut from the garden, plus a few leftover 'Purple Tiger' (above) and 'Café Latte' roses from The Real Flower Company (see Sources, pages 204–205). I arrange the flowers in an old silver bowl using a pin frog and chicken wire held in place with floral tape, allowing the stems to fall naturally as they might do in the garden at this of year.

URN OF PLENTY

I don't prune my roses hard in winter – I leave them long so that I can cut generous stems in late summer, as here with David Austin's *Rosa* 'Gentle Hermione' (opposite). They give proportion and a feeling of generosity to the arrangement by adding height, and are reminiscent of fluffy clouds on a summer's day. 'Champagne Moment' and 'The Lark Ascending' roses fill the bottom of the urn, while the warm yellow tones continue off to the left with a couple stems of *Calendula officinalis* 'Touch of Red Buff' searching for the light. I tuck in a couple of *Dahlia* 'Cornel Brons' and a 'Wine Eyed Jill' (see also above) down into the arrangement. A stem of dried *Limonium gmelinii* fills the space on the right-hand side, while a single strand of wild hedgerow *Humulus lupulus* wraps around the base of the urn, anchoring the urn to the table.

BEAUTY CAUGHT IN TIME
My guilty pleasure is finding a jar of dried-out flowers abandoned on a shelf in the studio. These ranunculus were originally bright orange, while the red dahlia heads date back to the autumn before (opposite). Like this *Hydrangea paniculata* 'Limelight' (left), they have had no special treatment. In fact, their papery petals are the result of utter neglect and lack of water.

ELEVATING THE SIMPLE

Drying flowers

LATE SUMMER IS THE PERFECT TIME OF YEAR TO DRY FLOWERS. If you are organized, like my friend Carol, you will have planned for this moment and considered the quantities of flowers you might need when planning your planting. You will have thought about interesting seed heads, and what might be popular with florists looking for inspiration throughout the long winter months.

Once again, there is a growing trend within the floral industry for dried flowers. It has taken some time for the image of a dusty jug of brittle dried blooms to be reinvented in our consciousness, but why wouldn't you want to enjoy your dahlias throughout the winter, long after the first frosts have drawn a final curtain over this year's performance?

You can dry most flowers given the right conditions. Somewhere dry and dark, to avoid bleaching of colours by the sun – although to be honest, I rather favour the muted look. When you cut blooms, keep the stems as long as possible. Tie them into bunches, hang them upside down in a well-ventilated place and watch. It can be addictive after a while, and some of the most fascinating results are achieved by accident.

Occasionally, I come across jars of cut flowers that were forgotten while waiting for their moment to be arranged. But somehow time got the better of me. When the jars are finally rediscovered, the flowers have either turned into black, slimy heaps that need immediate eviction to the compost heap, or have dried up completely. Slightly reproachful, and with an air of Miss Havisham about them, they give me great joy for many months to come with their fragile beauty and almost transparent tissue-paper petals.

MY LATE SUMMER STUDIO

I hang cut stems of flowers to dry upside down from hooks in the studio ceiling (left), but you can get beautiful results popping one or two stems in a vase to drink themselves dry (above). Try hydrangea heads or roses and experiment to see what works. To dry larger amounts of flowers, strip the leaves off the stems, tie them into small bunches with string and hang them upside down (right). They need a warm, dry room out of direct sunlight and with plenty of air circulation. Don't be tempted to tie large bunches, as they won't get enough air and will go mouldy in the middle. Limonium, or statice, dries beautifully, but it does smell of rotting fish during the process, so possibly move that one out of the studio and into the garden shed!

AN EVERLASTING ARRANGEMENT

For those who don't fancy attaching dried flowers
to the wall (see overleaf), here is an option for
a table arrangement using dried flowers and
a vintage glass flower frog to hold the stems.
A frog is a glass sphere with a flat bottom and
holes in the sides that I push the dried stems into
and hold in place, if needed, with floral fix. Using
a similar palette to the wall bouquet, I have
included *Lunaria annua var. albiflora* (honesty),
larkspur, limonium, *Stipa tenuissima* 'Pony Tails',
Lathyrus latifolius (perennial sweet pea), the
grey wispy flower heads of *Perovskia* 'Blue Spire'
and dried dahlia heads from Justdahlias (see
Sources, pages 204–205)

AN EVERLASTING BOUQUET
Dried art

NOT ONLY DO DRIED FLOWERS MAKE THE MOST
SURPRISING SHAPES and reinvent themselves into simple works
of beauty without you even having to lift a finger, but they also last as long as
you want, depending on your taste for desiccated petals and tolerance for dust.
Elegant and ethereal, dried flowers work so well inside, and can be changed
seasonally to suit the season or your mood.

This late summer dried flower bouquet hangs on the wall and is not so
much an arrangement as an artwork that can change on a daily basis or even
be moved from room to room. It can be as simple or as complicated as desired.
I have used flowers from the garden, but they could be from local suppliers or
even foraged from the hedgerows. When you walk, whether in the city or on a
mountain, I urge you to look past the obvious.
Nature offers surprising beauty. Be mindful
of what you pick (and always ask first if it's in
someone else's garden).

BALLERINA CORNFLOWERS
Eager for any kind of colour back in April after a
long winter and cold spring, I potted up around
20 cornflowers in shades of pink. The seed packet
suggested a subtle pink, but Barbara Cartland in all
her glory came to stay. There was nothing demure
about this pink. They were all out for their moment in
the limelight. I gave them a week, then dug a few out
and hung them upside down (left). They remind me of
ballerina tutus.

You will need

✳ **Chicken wire or copper floral mesh**, a small tack hammer and a piece of wire and a picture hook.

✳ **Floral snips and a wire cutter** (never use your floral snips to cut wire, or you will blunt them).

flowers and stems

✳ **Focal and filler flowers x 10**, such as dahlias and dried rose heads in different sizes but similar tones.

✳ **Textural elements x a handful**. I have used small dried acer leaves to soften the edges plus smaller stems of *Stipa tenuissima* 'Pony Tails', lunaria (honesty) seedheads and *Perovskia* 'Blue Spire'.

✳ **Gestural moments x 2 or 3**. Dried long vines such as *Lathyrus latifolius* (perennial pea) and *Clematis vitalba* (old man's beard). These will give your arrangement its graceful shape.

step 1

Mould a piece of chicken wire measuring around 30 x 30cm/12 x 12in into a dome shape with a flat back so that it will sit flush against a wall. Fix a picture hook into the wall and attach the wire dome. Dried flowers aren't heavy, so the fixing doesn't need to be huge.

step 2

Using long pieces of perennial sweet pea, I start to build up the shape I want to create, always considering how the finished installation will look and relate to its surroundings. These fine tendrils are important, as they will stop the finished piece looking heavy or bulky.

step 3

I continue to cover the chicken
wire base with, in this case, a few
branches of dried acer leaves.

I love creating
a 'moment' on
the wall.

step 4

Start to break up the surface so
that it doesn't look flat. Here, I've
added a variety of dried dahlia
heads. You don't need many large
heads, as they will dominate,
rather like having too many divas
on stage at one time. Instead, use
smaller dahlias to form a cluster, a
place for your eye to pause.

step 5

Continue to build up layers, repeating colours throughout the piece. I've softened things up and added more texture in the shape of some fluffy *Clematis vitalba* (old man's beard) seed heads below the cluster of dahlias. Use colour in layers and mass it in certain areas to avoid ending up with definite colour blocks, otherwise the arrangement will look too busy.

step 6

A few delicate, silvery strands of *Perovskia* 'Blue Spirc' add interest and balance to the upper left-hand corner.

step 7

I'm not including bright colours in this piece, but I've used *Lunaria annua var. albiflora* (honesty) to lighten up areas that feel a bit dark, as well as some *Stipa tenuissima* 'Pony Tails' just off-centre under the large dahlia. *Lunaria* is a favourite of mine – I can lose myself peeling the papery covers off to reveal the silvery seed pods beneath. Keep on building up the arrangement until you are happy with the final shape.

step 8

And there you have it. A piece of artwork that will remind you of your summer garden. I've added a piece of ribbon, dyed by Ros from The Natural Dyeworks (see Sources, pages 204–205) to complete the image. It grounds the piece and takes it from rustic to something more glamorous – and we all need glamour in our lives.

We all need a bit of glamour in our lives.

AUTUMN

a season of change and curiosity

'You can't stop time. You can't capture the light. You can only turn your face up and let it rain down.'

KIM EDWARDS, *The Memory Keeper's Daughter*

CONNECTING TO THE LANDSCAPE

THE LIGHT SLOWLY CHANGES IN AUTUMN, ALMOST IMPERCEPTIBLY AT FIRST.

When the children go back to school, the jumpers come out of the box from under the bed, are checked for moth holes and either put to one side to darn or back in the box to deal with another time, because it's obvious that the moths have been eating out every night on my woollens, and my darning just isn't that good. And then – these days, these years – often the weather becomes warmer again. Just as if summer had a better offer in another part of the world, flew off on a jet plane for the whole of August, then suddenly remembered she had promised to come back for her swansong.

BURNISHED HUES
In autumn, Newby Hall gardens in Yorkshire (opposite) turn to burnished gold and copper with trees and foliage taking centre stage, while the sunflowers look as if they have dragged their sorry heads home from an all-night party (right).

The Garden

THE GARDEN FEELS AS IF SHE HAS EXHALED DEEPLY. She is at ease, loosening the top button of the silk skirt that has been just a little too tight all summer. She may slouch a little, battered by summer rain and tired from a recent storm, but she retains all her graceful elegance. The low sun shines through leaves that glisten with heavy morning dew, holding a day full of promise and possibility ahead.

I spend a few weeks at the beginning of October trying to hold onto the last of summer. The shortening days make me wistful for the long, balmy summer evenings that seemed to stretch on forever. Wearing a pair of glitter socks and the husband's wellies, I shuffle around the wet and soggy garden in a state of melancholy until I remember, usually sometime around mid-October, that autumn is possibly my favourite season and I'm missing all the best bits.

Before the winds come along and blow them all off, there are a few weeks where the trees hang heavy with leaves in tones of copper and plum. Viburnums, acers, forest pansies, amelanchiers and purple prunus all gleam in the afternoon sun, and there is something reassuringly familiar about the smell of woodsmoke on the air, the bejewelled carpets of leaves and the apple windfalls that are scooped up to make cider. The seasons are changing, whether I'm ready or not.

I briefly mourn the loss of abundance in the garden, but take great joy from discovering that the pots of chrysanthemums that I took cuttings from in the spring, and which have looked rather uninspiring for most of the year, are having a moment. Unstaked and suffering from neglect, they have fallen sideways and grown at strange angles. I cut them and bring them inside for a burst of colour.

I am excited about making plant dyes from the natural harvest and creating some images using the last of the flowers in the garden. Autumn is good for me. I allow myself some time to sit and reflect, dream and collect – and make a mental note that I really must clean the windows.

There is a Japanese acer in a pot on the patio that I just know would look wonderful if only I could drag it inside and photograph it. But it's heavy, and is giving me a look that says, 'I'm quite happy here thank you. If you move me inside, anywhere near a whiff of central heating, I'm going to shed all my leaves. Yep, just like that.' I decide to have another coffee and think about it. Maybe I'll collect some leaves instead.

While I waft around the garden picking up fallen leaves and marvelling at their glorious colours, the husband is set on clearing the gutters. He drags the rickety old ladder out of the shed, grumbling about the leaves wedged in the downpipes that are causing water to stream down the outside of the house. I leave him hauling them out and dumping them in buckets that are attached to the ladder with pieces of twine. Oh dear – I shouldn't have left the foot of the ladder. Then it wouldn't have slipped, and the husband

SOFTLY, SOFTLY

The light becomes softer in autumn, but there is still a warmth in the air and the plants in the herbaceous borders take on muted jewel tones. In the gardens of Newby Hall, the sun just peeps through the clouds, throwing an ethereal, misty haze across the late-flowering asters, salvias and pretty pinky purple-flushed *Dahlia* 'Bishop of Dover' (above and left).

wouldn't have fallen…using my beautiful acer to break his fall. He appears at the kitchen door, looking slightly battered and bruised. I am somewhat distracted by the number of interesting leaves attached to his head, but arrange my face into an expression of concern, until I notice that he clutches the branch – the main branch, in fact all of the tree, my beautiful acer tree – in his hand, like the staff of a mountain warrior.

'Are you OK?' I ask, my eyes darting swiftly to the tree.

'Yes,' he says, looking cheerful. 'Good job that tree was there, it broke my fall. Not much of it left though I'm afraid.'

'Well,' I say, 'At least you're OK. Have a cup of tea.'

'Where are you going?' he replies, peeling leaves off his head.

'I just need to immortalize this branch in a photograph,' I sigh. 'She was so lovely.'

DRAMATIC BEAUTY

You don't need oodles of flowers to make a statement arrangement, especially in autumn. A branch like this one from an acer tree will last for a good week, possibly even two (depending on how hot you like to keep your house) in a large bucket or urn of water (opposite). I'm not suggesting that you cut off large limbs of trees, simply make the most of any windfallen boughs or branches.

FALL COLOURS

The warm, inviting and enveloping colours of autumn foliage and late perennials turning deep vermillion, rich saffron and ochres are a sight to behold – and a florist's dream (pages 124–125). The cascading branches of *Euonymus europaeus*, or the spindle tree, come into their own in autumn (above). The leaves turn rich reds and the small flowers of summer become orange and pink winged fruits, reminding me of old-fashioned boiled sweets. Other autumn favourites include *Rudbeckia hirta* 'Sahara', which is a staple in my autumn flower beds. I sow them from seed early in March, impatient for their muted pink and caramel tones to appear in late September and last all the way through to the frosts (opposite above left). There's also *Acer palmatum* 'Osakazuki', which is a superb large shrub or small tree for most sized gardens and has leaves that turn a brilliant scarlet in autumn (opposite above right). Also appearing at this time of year is *Dahlia* 'Mango Madness' doing her crazy whirling dance (opposite below right), while the leaves of the blueberry bush turn a deep, sultry carmine (opposite below left).

IMPERFECTION

'THE SECRET OF WABI SABI LIES IN SEEING THE WORLD NOT WITH A LOGICAL MIND, BUT THROUGH A FEELING HEART. IT IS AN INTUITIVE RESPONSE TO BEAUTY THAT REFLECTS THE TRUE NATURE OF LIFE.'

BETH KEMPTON, *WABI SABI – JAPANESE WISDOM FOR A PERFECTLY IMPERFECT LIFE*

I had always assumed that wabi sabi was the right description for an imperfect object with a story to tell. A 19th-century urn with chipped feet, perhaps. A textured wall with a wonderful patina created by years of decay. An old toy dog with an ear missing and the stuffing leaking out. Imperfect objects.

With an antiques dealer father, who brought home all sorts of treasures on a weekly basis, I always gravitated towards objects made hundreds of years ago. I felt uncomfortable with the shiny, mass-marketed products in high-street shops, and was instead fascinated by the imperfections wrought by time – the derelict house that needed more than just a makeover, or an old table with its layers of chipped gloss paint telling of multiple previous lives. However, I was missing the point. I was focused on the object itself, the acquisition of it and not my response to it.

SEASONAL TREASURES
Due to pretty poor staking attempts in the garden, *Chrysanthemum* 'Allouise Orange' is rain-battered and growing sideways (above). I pick a handful nonetheless and pop them in an earthenware jug for a splash of vibrant autumnal colour in the kitchen (opposite above). Ted the cat promises to rouse himself from sleep to admire them at some point.

Chasing perfection

IT IS NO SECRET THAT THE MODERN WORLD CONSIDERS a brilliant, interesting and successful person, possibly worthy of superhero status, one who is constantly engaged in a whirl of relentless productivity that results in glamorous homes, new clothes, perfect teeth and pampered pets.

In my search for an outwardly perfect life, I would rise before dawn to watch the sunrise but forget to do that as I instead answered the impressively large number of emails lying in our inbox. I must fit in a quick jog before breakfast, feeding the animals and levering the teenager out of bed in time to catch the school bus. It's time for a quick post on social media, but I missed the sunrise as I was busy answering emails, so I decide to get the cat to pose instead. But first the cat needs a brush, as he has spent the night in the weed patch and is covered in sticky bobs. I am so busy trying to get the cat to pose that the teenager misses the school bus and I have to drive him to school, abandoning my planned breakfast of antioxidant-rich fruits and freshly pressed apple juice and grabbing a piece of dry toast. And so I am late for a meeting in a field to appraise the possibility of turning it into a country park for a client and installing two lakes, all the time hopefully looking super-efficient while surreptitiously trying to remove sticky bobs from my hair and toast crumbs from my jacket. Next, it's time to whizz home to dye 20 linen sheets with dahlia flower heads, make some hand-printed paper before lunch and create a perfect image to post on social media before dinner.

This quest for worthiness left me exhausted and anxious, constantly chasing society's version of perfection. I felt guilty if I took a moment to simply be still. Was 10 minutes spent roaming around the garden in the morning a slip down the ladder? Perhaps taking the time to notice the changing seasons was a waste of precious time that I could have used more productively?

I agonized over an afternoon spent arranging flowers. Were they perfect enough to post on social media? What was perfect anyway? Was I enjoying the precious moments creating the arrangement, or feeling guilty because I should be dusting the house instead? If the arrangement turned out to be slightly less than perfect, it would be a waste of an afternoon, as it wouldn't be going anywhere near social media. In which case, the dusting would be a better option. Was I overthinking everything? Yes, I was, and it was making me unhappy. So I decided to give myself permission to take time for the small moments, and to take note of the feelings that nature's transient beauty evoked in me.

Accepting imperfection

FOR ME, AUTUMN IS THE EMBODIMENT OF WABI SABI. As a season she slows and ponders, and encourages us to embrace the stillness and listen to our personal conversations with the landscape.

As I squelch across the sodden lawn towards the cutting beds, I take time to pause and look – really look – ignoring the rain plastering my hair to my face. The last of the roses are rain-freckled, excess water mottling the outer petals from blush to a watercolour hue. A clematis leaf has been bleached by the wind and change in temperature, a rudbeckia is ragged around the edges and rows of echinaceas catch the last of the fading light, a few petals hanging from their seed heads. I feel peaceful and ready for a change in pace.

I collect the last of the beans, now uneatable but a splendid shade of bruised plum and fawn, and cut a few long, willowy strands of perennial sweet pea. It has dried to a bleached and papery hue, but if anything has become more elegant and refined in decay. This cheers me immensely. I wonder if perhaps I can become more elegant and refined in my old age? Probably just papery and clinging tightly to anything that keeps me upright, but possibly…I just need to be my authentic self, before I forget what it is I'm supposed to be clinging to.

AMAZING GREY

Normally blooming in June, this *Papaver rhoeas* 'Amazing Grey' was a late self-seeder (left). Slightly battered by the rain and her papery petals nipped by the wind at the edges, she was quietly doing her thing in the middle of the dahlia bed. 'You go girl,' I said. 'Looking good.' She gave me a knowing look. 'Yup,' she said, 'loving it…wish I'd brought a coat though.' She sighed happily, then all her petals fell off.

FALLEN LEAVES

As the light fades and I enjoy the garden in all her new-found abandon, I look beyond the boundaries for inspiration. I want to collect fallen leaves in all their vermillion, ruby and gingerbread tones and preserve some so that I can soak up their vibrancy on the dreary days ahead. We go for walks along the lanes with the dogs. Childhood memories of kicking leaves in wellington boots give me a burst of energy, until the husband reminds me that we live in a highly dog-populated area and those mounds of leaves might be hiding a less-than-fragrant surprise (right).

TAKING NATURE INSIDE

I GREW UP IN THE CITY, ON THE OUTSKIRTS OF SOUTH-EAST LONDON. I FOUND IT LOUD, DEMANDING AND SOMETIMES CLAUSTROPHOBIC.

I rarely stopped to look up or even look down – I was too busy being busy. I didn't pause to look past the person in front, or beyond the traffic straight ahead.

I didn't see that nature in all her glory was quietly biding her time, there for all who cared to look and offering as much delight and beauty as any flashy shop selling the latest must-have merchandise. Nature gives us fresh perspective daily, and if you are open to it, she offers a calm beauty amid the dusty chaos of city life.

Nowadays I give myself permission to slow down when I visit the city – any city. To see beyond the sad-looking shrubs that have been sculpted into unspeakable shapes by the local council, the graceful arch of a branch whipped away, the flower nipped in the bud. If you look up, you will spot shrubs and climbers that have escaped our desire to make them tidy and spherical. They are having a lovely time doing their own natural thing and the effect is awe-inspiring. I encourage you to look up.

LIVING WALLPAPER
I spotted this Virginia creeper (*Parthenocissus quinquefolia*) hanging from the trees over the pavement in the city of York (above). More often found growing up the side of a house, here she cascades from the trees in all her autumn glory like sumptuous lengths of velvet and silk ribbons, decadent with not a care in the world. Inspired, on my return home I make a visit to a friend who I know has the creeper growing wildly in her garden and snip a few long strands. I place the stems in water tubes and attach to a hook in the ceiling in my studio (opposite). Never has wallpaper looked so good!

STAR PERFORMERS

Rosa 'The Lark Ascending' is the most diligent rose in my garden (above left). Flowering her socks off in early June, she just gets better and better through the season. Apricot blooms fade into a soft rose edged with buttercream as the seasons progress. The large-headed *Dahlia* 'Café au Lait' needs a big urn to do her justice, as she is a bit of an extrovert and likes full attention (above right).

AUTUMNAL ABUNDANCE

By autumn, the roses have softened in colour and the stems become compliant, allowing you to drape them over the sides of an urn (opposite). The heart-shaped leaves of *Cercis canadensis* (forest pansy) turn shades of magenta and plum, and I tuck a stem in the right of the urn. She is quite dominant and could make the urn feel unbalanced, so I increase the number of roses, acer foliage and small dahlia heads to the left. Dried stems of pink larkspur unite the image. I softly drape a length of dyed linen across a box. She has her cape on and is ready for her moment on the stage.

USING FOLIAGE IN ARRANGEMENTS

The abundance of flowers in the garden slows down by late October, so I use a lot of majestic and dramatic autumnal foliage found in the garden in my arrangements. Acer trees become warm, tumbling waterfalls of coppers, reds and bronzes (top), while the peony leaves also have a rather lovely silver underside to them that I sometimes use as a highlight if an arrangement becomes too muted (above). A *Macleaya microcarpa* or plume poppy flower (shown reaching for the sky in the urn) offers a light, feathery moment and ekes out some late roses and a handful of dahlias (opposite).

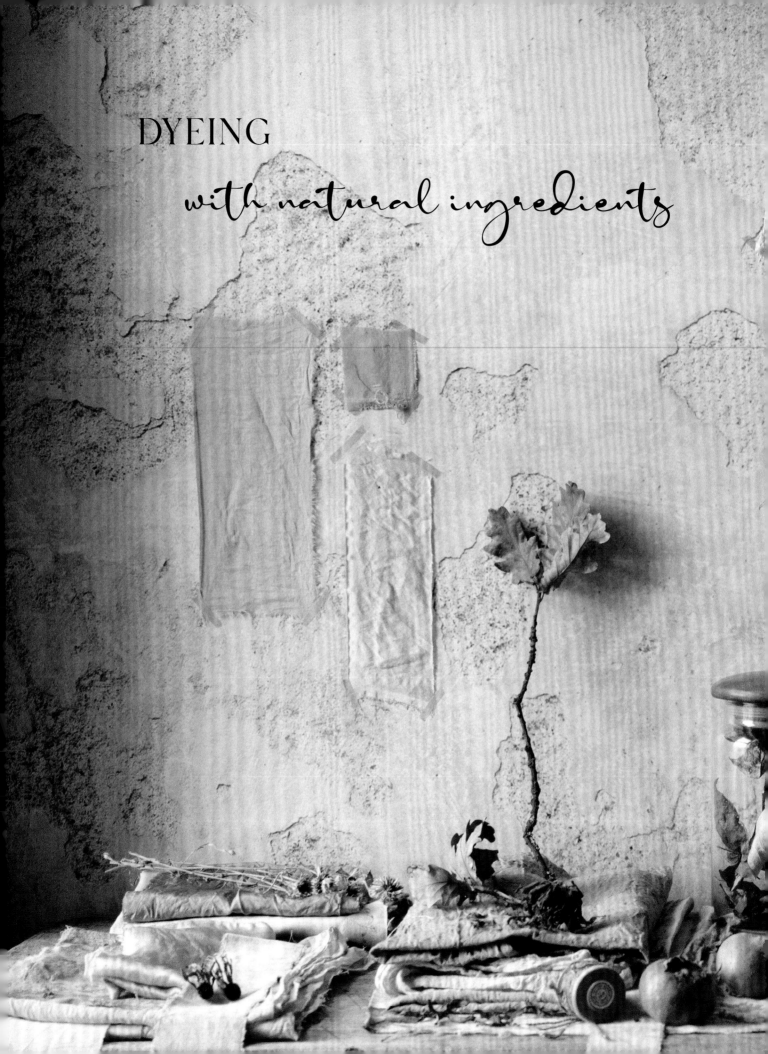

DYEING

with natural ingredients

I WOULDN'T DESCRIBE MYSELF AS A DYE EXPERT, BUT AN ENTHUSIAST. To produce the perfect silk ribbon for a bride's day takes a great deal of patience and a fair amount of skill, and I always had a worrying lack of focus in the chemistry lab at school. If I need long lengths of silk ribbon to wrap around a bride's bouquet, then I enlist professional help from one of the talented craftspeople who have spent many hours honing their skills (see Sources, pages 204–205).

However, my desire to see what colours I can produce from the flowers and weeds that grow under my nose in the garden is a temptation too great for me to resist. The basic process isn't difficult and you can dye at all times of the year, using dye made from natural ingredients foraged in the landscape or your own garden. It leaves me fascinated and the husband tearing his hair out, as the kitchen range resembles something you might expect to see at Hogwarts.

There is something lovely about growing flowers and vegetables during the summer, savouring your hard toil in delicious meals, enjoying the flowers in a vase, and then using their pigments to dye fabric glorious colours. Any leftover dye is poured into the compost and then goes back into the soil, completing the circle.
Rose petals can be kept and dried or, even better, used fresh. Try the deep reds and pinks of *Rosa* 'Night Owl' to obtain purple pinks and light reds.

Japanese acers and prunus leaves, collected in autumn, give wonderful vintage rose and red shades.
Bracken gives an ochre green tone, while *Daucus carota* (wild carrot, or Queen Anne's lace) will give you light yellows and greens.
***Centaurea cyanus* 'Black Ball'** (cornflower) is easy to grow from seed in early summer and produces beautiful purpley blue shades.
Red onion skins transform silk into shimmering orangey-bronzed hues.
Pomegranates are surprising. You'd assume they would create a deep red dye that's the same colour as the skin, but no, a lovely golden bronze.
Aloe leaves, or the red flowers of amaranth, create the softest blush tones.
Avocados turn silks and linen to the palest, softest blush. Use the cleaned skins and stones.

Some seed companies now offer seeds for flowers that are particularly good for dyeing. Have a look and see what appeals to you (see Sources, pages 204–205). Bear in mind that your colours will vary depending on the pH of the water and, it would appear, where in the world you are growing your flowers. But it is fascinating to experiment – have fun with it.

PERFECT PLANTS FOR DYE
The muted plum tones of *Prunus cerasifera* 'Nigra' shimmer in the late autumn sun (opposite above). They make a beautiful dye rather like a pale blackberry jam/jelly. *Tagetes patula* 'Burning Embers' and *Coreopsis tinctoria* planted en masse in my friend Carol's garden (opposite below).

A basic guide to dyeing your own fabrics at home

THIS IS THE WAY I MAKE AND USE MY OWN DYES, BUT THERE ARE MANY MORE IN-DEPTH BOOKS AND WEBSITES ON DYEING AVAILABLE IF YOU WISH TO INVESTIGATE FURTHER.

You will need

✳ Fabric (or a garment) for dyeing. I would suggest using an organic cotton, wool or silk fabric that hasn't been bleached or pre-dyed.

✳ Liquid soap

✳ Scales for weighing your fabric and your chosen mordant

✳ Mordant for plant fibres (e.g. cotton, linen and hemp): oak gall extract powder or aluminium acetate.

✳ Mordant for animal fibres (e.g. wool, silk): alum (potassium aluminium sulphate) (approx. 2 tbsp for one small item), plus cream of tartar.

✳ A large clean pot. I use my mum's old marmalade-making pan – you can pick up ones like this on Etsy or ebay. Do not use the same pot that you'll be cooking dinner in.

✳ A heat source. When you are 'mordanting' (see page 146), it is advisable to have good ventilation. If your kitchen is not suitable, you can buy an inexpensive portable gas stove and mordant your fabric outside.

✳ A wooden spoon

✳ Flowers, bark or leaves to make the dye

✳ A colander or sieve

✳ pH-neutral soap

step 1

PREPARE YOUR FABRIC

Wash and scour your fabric first, using an eco-friendly liquid soap. You'll be amazed how dirty even seemingly clean fabric is. Leave it to dry, then weigh the fabric in its dry state.

step 2

MORDANTING THE FABRIC

The word 'mordant' comes from the Latin word *mordere*, meaning to bite or bite into. Mordanting the fabric allows the fibres to open up and take (or bite into) the dye, resulting in stronger and brighter colours. It also helps to reduce fading.

PLANT FIBRES

Plant fibres such as cotton, linen and hemp must be mordanted with a plant-based mordant that is high in tannic acid, like extract of oak galls, chestnuts, acorns and other nuts and barks. Use 1 teaspoon of oak gall extract powder for every 100g/3½oz of dry fabric weight. Alternatively, you can use aluminium acetate, in which case measure out 5–10% of the weight of the dry fabric. Dissolve your chosen mordant in water, then bring it to the boil in a large pan. Add the fabric and make sure it is fully immersed by pushing it down with a wooden spoon. Bring the water back to the boil, then turn off the heat and allow the pan and its contents to cool for 12 hours. Make sure this process takes place in a well-ventilated room. Open the windows wide or turn on the extractor fan.

ANIMAL FIBRES

Animal fibres such as wool and silk must be mordanted with a plant-based mordant that is high in toxic oxalic acid, like extract of rhubarb leaves. A quicker, easier and safer option is to use alum (potassium aluminium sulphate). Measure out 8% of the weight of the dry fabric in alum, and 7% in cream of tartar, and dissolve the crystals and powder in enough water to cover the fabric, then bring it to the boil in a large pan. Add the fabric and make sure it is immersed by pushing it down with a wooden spoon. Bring the water back to the boil and simmer for an hour, stirring every so often. If you are dyeing wool, watch the temperature like a hawk. Over-enthusiastic boiling on my part has resulted in lots of jumpers that now only fit the cat!

step 3

MAKING THE DYE

Creating a dye from a flower, root or foraged material is rather like making tea – simply steep your materials, chopped if you are using large flowers or leaves or bark, in boiling water for a least an hour. Here, I picked a handful of coreopsis heads from Carol's garden and popped them in the pan to see luscious pale gold pigments slowly emerging as the flowers infuse. If you don't have natural materials to hand, you can always buy natural plant dye powders (see Sources, pages 204–205). Now strain out the plant material before using the dye bath.

step 4

THE DYE BATH

If you have taken your eye off the pan during the extraction process, you may find the water level has dropped due to evaporation. If so, add more water – enough so that your fabric will be able to move easily around the pan. Now add the mordanted fabric. Bring the pan to the boil, then reduce the heat and simmer, stirring regularly, for an hour. Remove the pan from the heat, pour your fabric into a colander or sieve and rinse it in lukewarm water. Wash using a pH-neutral soap, then allow it to air-dry.

step 5

MODIFIERS

After you have dyed your fabric, if desired you can
alter the colour using a modifier. Acidic modifiers,
such as lemon juice, vinegar or tannic acid, will shift
the colour towards yellow, orange or red. Alkaline
modifiers, such as iron solution, make colours greyer
or more muted. Be careful – too much iron solution
will turn your creation black. Which is lovely if you
want black, but not if you're aiming for a muted shade
of moss green. I share this through bitter experience.

step 6

Once a dyed fabric is dry, I cut a patch and stick a
sample in my journal, noting the exact ingredients
for future reference (see overleaf). I often use the
fabric to cover notebooks or cut it into strips (above)
and wrap around old vintage cotton reels for use as
ribbons on bouquets of flowers or presents for friends.

Linen and Silk.
Mordant with
    Acorns
overdyed with
    Amaranth.

TURNING THE PAGES

In my journals, I record the results of my dyeing experiments (this page and opposite). It is so easy to forget how you obtained that colour that was just the right shade of blush, so my notes are invaluable. I also like to include vintage floral cotton fabrics with French linens and aged silver thread. In an old box that I covered with a remnant of antique French toile de Jouy, I keep dyed silk ribbons wrapped on old cotton reels (opposite above right). Sometimes in late winter, when all the colour seems to have disappeared from the landscape, I like to take a peek inside the box. It reminds me to look forward to the seasons ahead.

Linen, Silk, Velvet
Dyes: foraged leaves
    from the garden
Mordant; None

Linen, Silk and Velvet.
Mordant Alum and
Oak Galls
Dye; Coreopsis
Modified, weak iron
bath.

Black hollyhock
by
The Natural Dye
Works

Red Cabbage
by
The Natural
Pigments.

Silk.
Mordant, Alum and
Cream of tartar.

Dye, Black cornflowers

BRINGING THE OUTSIDE IN

an autumnal urn

THE SHEER ABUNDANCE OF THE AUTUMN GARDEN MAKES IT HEAVEN FOR FLOWER ARRANGERS. There is never a better time to create a dramatic 'spilly' urn overflowing with flowers and foliage cut from the garden. Forage for branches dripping with berries or hips, or shrubs with foliage that boasts amazing autumnal hues. Roses, full blown and slightly battered by the cooler weather, add wonderful texture and interest. The shapes in this particular arrangement should be relaxed and inviting – it's all about the elegant slump.

PLAYING SHOPS

I had romantic notions of being a shopkeeper when I was a child. I dreamed of tall counters covered with antique objects from another time, and paintings and silks that visitors would gasp over. Then I realized that I actually just liked arranging objects and flowers to make an emotive image. So this is my shopfront, offering up acers, roses, chrysanthemums, dahlias, rudbeckias, crimson amaranth, plum sedums, a few gourds and a pink pumpkin (left).

flowers and stems

✳ **Structural branches x 3 or 4.** Look for branches with leaves that are changing colour, such as *Physocarpus opulifolius* 'Diabolo' or *Cotinus coggygria* (smoke bush).

✳ **Filler flowers x 4 or 5 stems.** The last of the garden roses are big and generous. I'm using *Rosa* 'Desdemona'.

✳ **Focal flowers x 15.** I'm using the last of the autumn dahlias and *Chrysanthemum* 'Allouise Salmon'.

✳ **Gestural moments x a handful.** These wispy stems will give your arrangement a final flourish. I have snipped a few stems of *Euonymus europaeus* (spindle tree), *Stipa tenuissima* 'Pony Tails' and acer leaves.

You will need

✳ **A suitable vessel.** Use whatever feels right for you, but bear in mind that an urn or vase with a wide, low rim will allow flowers to tumble loosely over the side.

✳ **A piece of rubber pond liner**

✳ **Floral fix and floral tape**

✳ **Chicken wire and/or a floral pin frog** to hold heavy stems in place.

✳ **Floral snips**

step 1 and 2

Choose your vessel or urn, thinking carefully about the desired shape of the arrangement. Here, I'm using a wide urn that allows the flowers to gracefully tumble over the sides. None of my urns are watertight, so I've used an offcut of rubber pond liner to line this one. Using floral fix, I attach a floral frog to the bottom to hold heavy stems in place. Now cut a piece of chicken wire to fit into the urn and secure it with floral tape.

TURNING LEAVES
Autumn foliage plays a leading role in this urn. Look for leaves that are mottled by the rain or slightly frostbitten. Sometimes you can find a branch with an amazing shape or graceful curve if you look below or at the back of the shrub (opposite).

step 3

Once the urn is filled with water, I start to add the structural branches. Here, I'm using *Physocarpus opulifolius* 'Diabolo' to create a sweeping shape on the left. This is an easy-to-grow shrub that favours a well-drained ground. It has small pinky-white flowers in summer, but I like it for its deep burgundy foliage, which softens slightly in the autumn and produces a range of browns and reds before the leaves fall off. It can have quite stiff, upright stems, but older stems at the base of the shrub tend to have a longer, more graceful shape. Next, I push in some *Cotinus coggygria* 'Royal Purple' to the right – another fabulous shrub much loved by florists. It produces hazy plumes in summer, hence its common name of smoke bush.

step 4

I continue to add pieces of foliage at the sides, building up a bit of drama and adding contrast with the yellowing leaves of *Cercidiphyllum japonicum*. I am keeping the middle section quiet, so there is space for small focal flowers.

Build up drama and contrast.

step 5

My filler flowers are *Rosa* 'Desdemona'. I grow as many roses as I can and use them from June through to late October, but if you are going to plant just one shrub rose in your garden, then 'Desdemona' is the one. When arranging the roses, I look at the way they hang before I add them to the urn. I want them to appear as if they are tumbling over a wall in wild abandon.

step 6

I place a few smaller pink rosettes of *Rosa* 'Cornelia' to the left-hand side to catch the light and break up the hard lines of the structural branches.

step 7

To balance the structure, I push in a sprig of *Euonymus europaeus* (spindle tree) berries to draw the eye to the right.

step 8

Now I start to add larger focal flowers, in this case dahlias. I want the arrangement to read from left to right, with colour, shape and form effortlessly carrying your eye across the arrangement as if it were a painting. Each flower needs room to breathe. Think about how plants look together in the garden. Which direction would they naturally grow? How would they reach for the light?

step 9

I continue to push in smaller flowers to fill gaps or soften harsh lines. Once the bulk of the arrangement is in place, I break up the lines of stems by adding wispy grasses and dried flowers, in this case a branch of pale yellow acer leaves to the left, a couple of strands of *Stipa tenuissima* 'Pony Tails' that look like a puff of smoke and two stems of dried astilbe flowers.

step 10

When you think you have finished, take a break. Go and make a cup of tea, then come back. It's amazing what you'll see with fresh eyes. Does the arrangement work proportionally? While it doesn't need to be symmetrical, it should be balanced.

step 11 (overleaf)

To finish, I have added a few luscious semi-double *Dahlia* 'Karma Fuchsiana' and a graceful strand of dried perennial sweet pea on the right, plus a handful of tomatoes scattered around the base of the urn in the manner of a Dutch still life. Now the urn is ready for its moment in the limelight. I have photographed it against a dark background, with the low autumn sun catching the vibrant pink of the dahlias.

WINTER

a season of extremes

'If you have built castles in the air, your work
need not be lost; that is where they should be.
Now put foundations under them.'

HENRY DAVID THOREAU, *Walden*

CONNECTING TO THE LANDSCAPE

THE GARDEN IS CARPETED BENEATH A THIN DUSTING OF SNOW AND ICE.

Finally she sleeps, restoring her energy under the soil and quietly making plans for the longer days ahead. I follow her lead and accept that time spent indoors, curled up in an old armchair by the kitchen window, is time well spent.

The snow makes the garden look quite serene. No mud, no decay – just peaceful and utterly quiet, apart from the occasional bird chirp. I go out to feed the chicken and break the ice on her water, and notice the fragile but determined snowdrops pushing their way up through the grass under the trees.

WINTER CHILL
We stay close to home in the cold, snowy days of winter. Old trees, mainly Scots pines, oaks, yew and beech, stand tall and whisper of stories from days gone by. Their noble, reassuring presence offers a sense of calm wisdom (opposite and right).

ICE SCULPTURES IN THE GARDEN

I don't cut down seed heads in winter, leaving them intact to feed hungry birds, and so I can enjoy wonderful the ice and frost sculptures that form around them. *Hydrangea arborescens* flower heads (above) have a fragile beauty, while the spidery blooms of *Hamamelis* x *intermedia* (witch hazel) look like tiny ribbons of wild silk and emit a warm, spicy scent, stopping you in your tracks on a snowy day (right). The orange tones echo the reddened stems of sedum (opposite above).

WINTER WARMERS

Gilbert the Welsh Whippet sports a hand-me-down coat from Wilson and an old wellington boot liner with the foot cut off as a neck ruff for our long winter walks (above right).

It's a small patch of snowdrops that I dug up from my grandmother's garden many years ago and which makes itself slightly bigger every year. I occasionally add bulbs from friends' gardens that are 'in the green' (snowdrops transplant far better if they are in the green rather than dry bulbs). A small bunch wrapped in newspaper is transported home, where I pot them up in a small bowl and enjoy the flowers inside for a week or so before planting them out in the garden for next year. Traditionally a sign of purity, snowdrops give me a renewed sense of optimism and remind me that nature carries on regardless of all the loud noise and general disagreement in the world.

The grasses and perennials have yet to be cut down in their beds, and the seed heads look like tiny jewels in the frost, each of them an exquisite sculpture made from ice. The rudbeckias in the cut-flower beds look as if they have had a wild night at a party and have just been caught dragging their sorry heads home.

And now I am going to take lessons from the cat, who lies in his basket next to the old armchair, fast asleep. Time to daydream is not time wasted. I take the opportunity to sit and stare for a while, considering the many possibilities that spring dangles like a carrot just over the horizon, and planning my planting dreams in the cutting garden.

A bowl of snowdrops

EARLY IN JANUARY, WHEN THE GARDEN IS
PREDOMINANTLY MUD BROWN, I bring some
snowdrops inside. They prefer the cool, damp soil
under the hedges and trees at the end of the garden,
but for just a few weeks I dig up a few small clumps
to plant in bowls and pots. I place them somewhere
cool in the house and am careful not to let them dry
out. Once they've finished flowering, they can go back
into the garden. Snowdrops can also be cut to strike
a delicate note in a small arrangement, but they don't
like the heat and won't last long in water, so I find them
better when they are left on the bulb.

A CARPET OF SNOWDROPS
Over time, snowdrops planted in a shady and rich but well-drained soil will self-seed and multiply into huge drifts of white that cover the ground (pages 168–169). To appreciate their fragile, otherworldly beauty, crouch down to their level and take a close look.

ETHEREAL CHARM
If you don't have snowdrops in your garden, you can buy small pots from the garden centre in early January and re-pot them in a small bowl or dish of your choice (opposite and above). They last about as long as a bunch of supermarket flowers and will strike a delicate, wintry note in any room. Such arrangements make a charming bedside display in a guest bedroom or even the perfect present.

A RIVER OF SCARLET
Schizostylis (kaffir lily) adds a wonderful addition of colour to the late winter garden when everything else looks brown and dreary. Here in The Laundry garden in North Wales, my friend Jenny has planted them in big, bold drifts that light up the winter sky (left). They last for at least a week when cut and placed in water.

EXOTIC BLOOMS
I hold my treasure aloft to admire the lipstick-red flowers born on long, thin stems. They will form the centrepiece of an arrangement that will grace our winter table (opposite above left).

The Garden

I FIND MYSELF FOLLOWING THE LOW WINTER SUN AROUND THE HOUSE as the year slowly draws to a close. I resist the shortening days, challenging myself instead to focus on an increasingly limited palette of garden flowers that I'm determined to arrange and photograph in natural daylight.

My neighbour and friend Jenny, who has a walled garden, calls to say she has some kaffir lilies, or *Schizostylis coccinea* 'Major', in flower. They love the reliably wet Welsh winters, well-drained soil and her warm, sun-drenched walls, and have grown into huge drifts, like a wide red river running through the bed – such a treat at this time of year. Would I like some when she digs them up to divide them in spring? Barely giving myself enough time to say, 'Yes please', I whizz over to see them before it gets too dark and Jenny can change her mind. We agree to a trade of a few photographs from me for a cut bunch now and a

FIERY COLOURS
In all their scarlet finery, the kaffir lilies become the star of the show in a small French drug jar filled with delicate winter offerings (right).

clump of tubers to plant later on. Cradling my treasure, I hurry back to the studio to get them into water, then make a small arrangement in an old drug jar.

Whether I'm designing a small vase for the table or a large urn for an installation, I always choose a focal flower first, then base my filler flowers around it. In the height of summer, when the garden is full to bursting and the roses are in full bloom, I have almost too much choice, and often I end up with too many focal flowers (or opera divas, as I like to call them). They jostle for the limelight and the arrangement looks unsettled. But today the kaffir lilies have my undivided attention. Red isn't a colour I use a lot during the rest of the year, and it can be difficult to photograph, but the flowers are crying out to be brought inside.

Deliberately keeping the rest of the palette limited, I snip a couple of roses that are just hanging on and haven't been pruned yet, some dried heather and strawflower, and a few wisps of *Clematis vitalba* (old man's beard). The jar has a narrow neck, so I push a small ball of chicken wire inside and fill it with water. I want to do justice to my diva, but I don't want her to dominate. The wispy dried pieces make the arrangement feel lighter and catch the last of the light.

It's after lunch, the afternoon sun has dropped and I realize that I'm working in semi-darkness. With a sigh, I switch on a lamp that throws a golden glow across the room. I wonder if the glow might thaw my frozen fingers and restore my dexterity. I plead my case for some extra heat in my studio as the number of jumpers

I'm wearing make useful body movement a dim and distant memory. The husband suggests lighting a fire in the grate. I dismiss this with an impassioned warning of a potential major calamity, pointing out all the dried flowers that artfully hang over and around the mantel.

As I stand and admire the wispy, delicate tendrils that speak to me of summer past, convinced that it is only a matter of moments before the husband admits his error and rushes out to buy me an electric heater, he suggests in a deceptively gentle tone that it would all make excellent kindling and he'll fetch the matches.

I'm left speechless and with my arms flapping like a penguin while I digest the horror of his suggestion and wonder how on earth I have been married for so long to a man who fails to see the enchantment in my wispy bits. He throws me another jumper on his way out.

THE BOUNTY OF THE WINTER GARDEN

You need to spend a bit of time rooting around for flowers and seed heads in the winter garden. But even when all looks cold, wet and miserable, there will still be something that you can use. Here, the kaffir lilies and dried *Calluna vulgaris* (heather) from the previous summer will be enough (opposite).

COLOUR AND TEXTURE

Winter is a time for appreciating the small treasures in your garden. You don't need a bucket of blooms to make a statement. My colour in this jar comes from the kaffir lilies, a few roses just clinging onto their petals, and a sprig of deep pink heather pushed down low. The rest is pulled together with the intriguing textures of pink pepperberry, *Clematis vitalba* (old man's beard) and lunaria (honesty) seed heads (above).

MY WINTER STUDIO
My studio in winter is crammed with various backdrops, antique jars, urns and a big table to work on. It can feel freezing in here during the colder months, but with a layers of woollies on and total focus on getting a few stems of *Daphne odora* 'Aureomarginata' to stay put in a tiny glass vase (opposite above), I don't feel the cold. Much.

THE STUDIO

A FEW SUMMERS BACK, WHEN THE
SUN BEAT FIERCELY DOWN AND THE
TEMPERATURE REMAINED A CONSTANT
26°C/79°F, I DECIDED THAT I NEEDED
MORE WALL SPACE.

The room my studio is based in forms part of the original section of the house, which was constructed in 1890 with flint and stone from the quarry on the mountain. Walls more than half a metre/nearly two feet thick and rendered with sand and cement stand firm, but without the insulation that today's building standards quite rightly insist upon. With no windows to speak of, only huge leaking skylights (the house was a Victorian hall designed to hold a huge billiard table that the Victorian gentleman would play on after dinner each night), I designed and we installed tall, generous windows and large double doors to lead out into the garden.

In summer, the sun pours through the windows all day and the thick walls keep the room cool. Flowers in cut buckets live for days. So during that warm week in summer, I forgot that the winters in North Wales are wet and bitterly cold, and we removed all the radiators in order to create more wall space for backdrops and pictures and shelves and flower stuff. The result is an amazing space with wonderful side light. It's perfect for arranging flowers, with big movable tables, plenty of storage space for equipment and tall walls from which to hang canvases and backdrops, resulting in flower arrangements that last for months...and occasional hypothermia in winter!

As well as teaching and designing here, the studio is the place I retreat to when I've consumed too much social media and coffee over breakfast, when it feels as if everyone else has a far better grip on this creativity malarkey and I am prey to the thought that enough is enough and I should really go and get a 'proper job'. It's where Wilson and I discuss the merits of tennis balls and why stealing my floral snips for his mud hole is not a favourable idea, while the Welsh Whippet chews a prized foraged branch of hedgerow with one perfectly imperfect leaf into a small pile of dust.

Here I record inspirations in my journals, stack backdrops against the walls, make a flowery mess and come to terms with the fact that while, possibly, I'm never going to become known for ground-breaking, never-before-considered art and flower arranging, the way I interpret the natural world will always be unique to me, just as it is to you.

OBJECTS
with a story to tell

WHEN I WAS ABOUT 12, MY FATHER RETIRED FROM TEACHING TO BECOME AN
ANTIQUES DEALER. HE WOULD SIGN UP FOR ANTIQUE FAIRS AND ON WEEKENDS
I WOULD GO WITH HIM TO SET UP HIS TABLE AND ARRANGE HIS 18TH-CENTURY
ORIENTAL PORCELAIN AND OTHER TREASURES.

I loved this job. I loved the exquisitely hand-painted Chinese famille rose plates and bowls, and dreamed about the stories they told of forgotten pasts. I would set up displays of old bowls on painted chests, gilded mirrors on tables and wooden carvings on books.

Eventually, after spending a few years in my late teens and early twenties wafting around with a paintbrush doing a Fine Art degree, listening to woeful music and feeling anguished, I decided that I needed to find a 'proper job'. One with a job title that would make people at parties nod their heads enthusiastically when I was asked, 'So what is it that you do?'

I abandoned my wistful mark-making, my old canvases were stored in the attic and I traded the paintbrushes for a pair of high heels and a suit and a nine-to-five job in a bank. I hated it and was pretty bad at it. The targets that I was set were intended to give me focus, but I rarely met any of them, as I was too busy staring out of the window at the tree tops opposite. I needed to be outside, I needed to be inspired with images and objects again and I wanted to find a way to mix the two.

And so I left the bank, retrained in garden design and started to bring my garden inside to fill the antique urns and bowls of my childhood. My arrangements were more than just a vase of flowers. They were a painting with objects chosen as a supporting cast, giving me the opportunity to relive precious childhood moments spent with my father.

TREASURED OBJECTS
Old pigments in jars and well-worn and well-loved paintbrushes in pots wait patiently for inspiration to strike (opposite above left); this 19th-century Swedish painting on linen is proof that you don't need to have a huge number of flowers to create a striking image (opposite above right); remnants of antique silk and brocade are piled together with freshly dyed linens (opposite below right); hand-beaded ribbons, quick sketches and silk flowers (opposite below left).

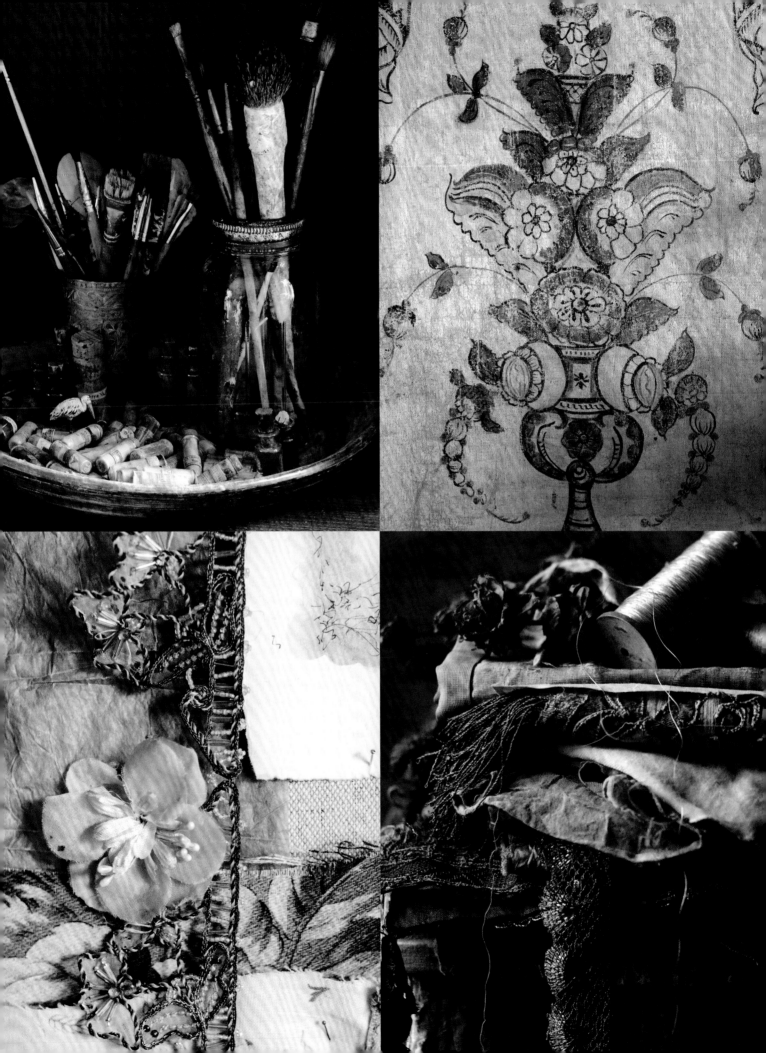

Urns and bowls

WHEN IT COMES TO CONTAINERS, I TEND TO CHOOSE OLD 19TH-CENTURY CAST-IRON URNS with simple yet graceful shapes that will support flowers in an artless, relaxed way. Antique urns like these are rarely waterproof, so I use rubber pond liner offcuts to line them. If they have a coat of old, chipped paint, so much the better – it gives them a time-worn character and a rich sense of individuality.

They are ridiculously heavy though, especially when filled with water, so after a few wedding seasons where I ended up with a slipped disc, I changed to smaller handmade ceramic bowls and now keep the cast-iron ones in the studio for teaching and photography. The simplicity of these urns and other metal vessels means the flowers can dominate. There is a tension between the simple and the complex that makes for a peaceful composition. Other containers, such as Delftware and Chinese porcelain vases, are more decorative and need a tonal palette. Your container is the supporting cast for your precious flowers, so plays an important role. High-street shops provide cheap cereal or soup bowls that are brilliant for flowers for the table, and I save glass jars in various sizes for small posies or conditioning stems. Think about your vessel. What shape and style particularly inspires or beguiles you?

FAVOURITE PROPS

Over the years, I have collected a number of props and objects that inspire and support the stories I tell in my images. I use tall stands as plinths for large urns that hold a mass of flowers, and shutters are invaluable for providing an interesting background, while chairs are always good for a sit-down (opposite).

CUT AND DRIED

A tiny 17th-century majolica pot can hold a surprising amount (above). Apart from a single rose just visible on the right-hand side, this arrangement is made up of dried flowers that I snipped from the garden in late summer, then hung up to dry, including hydrangea, helichrysum (strawflower), silvery elaeagnus and structural stems of oregano. I will enjoy her delicate beauty until she falls apart.

JAR OF DELIGHTS
Once I finish arranging this miniature jar, I compose my photograph (above and opposite). I want to emphasize the feeling of warmth and intimacy evoked by the spicy red tones of the kaffir lilies. Winter offers the perfect opportunity to make the most of the low light and create an image with the timeless feel of a Dutch still life. I carefully choose a backdrop – dark and textured – and fix it to the wall. Any ugly edges will be cropped out of the final edit. I adjust the exposure on my camera so that it's low, but not so low that the highlights of the glaze of the jar and on the flowers will be lost. Finally, I take the picture. It might become our Christmas card.

Paintings

I'M DRAWN TO PAINTINGS OF LANDSCAPES, SEASCAPES AND FLORAL MOTIFS, finding them in auction rooms, at old flea markets and through a few wonderful antiques dealers who uncover exquisite treasures (see Sources, pages 204–205). The paintings can be new or old, they don't have to be by a particular artist and they don't have to be worth very much. I am drawn to them purely because I like the colours and they invoke a sense of calm in me. They also work well as a prop within an image, and I sometimes use them to add supporting colour in the background. The size of the painting is considered, as well as the way that the edges break the space or frame or disrupt the composition and connect to the arrangement in the foreground.

fabrics and ribbons

I ADORE OLD FABRICS (which, the husband tells me, is why all my old jumpers are now moth-eaten). They seemed to use the finest silks and metallic threads years ago. Fragile but quite unique, such vintage fabrics add elusive texture to a bouquet or arrangement. Giving a nod to the past and to forgotten history, a delicate flower with glass beads will catch the light and give depth to an image. Newer silks, dyed as described in the previous chapter, add a sense of lightness. Contrasted with a heavy solid urn, they give an image a feeling of romance and anchor the vessel to the table, just as your garden should anchor your home within the landscape.

TEXTURAL TAPESTRY

A rich, dark backdrop with just the vaguest hint of texture is a perfect foil to a posy of dried flowers and a tiny fern leaf in a copper vase that has developed a layer of verdigris over time. This image was taken in the depths of winter, when anything still standing in the garden was frozen and covered in snow. But it is still possible to create an evocative image with a handful of dried flowers. The emphasis here is on texture, such as the feathery puffs of *Clematis vitalba* (old man's beard) drifting like smoke, and on the light bouncing off the silvery elaeagnus leaf and yellow senecio flowers (above).

Backdrops

I ALMOST ALWAYS USE BACKDROPS IN MY IMAGES, as described in the Spring chapter on page 45. Once upon a time, I had grand illusions of living in a wonderful chateau buried in deepest France and slowly crumbling into a state of romantic decay. The ballroom would have witnessed dancing late into the summer nights and overhead whispered gossip behind tall plaster columns. However, having just convinced the husband to spend all our money on a damp ruin on a Welsh mountain, those were dreams for another life. So I invested in and then started to paint my own backdrops, constructing my very own French chateau. These allow me to create a small stage set in the studio, acting as the perfect backdrop for arrangements.

Paper backdrops and murals can be bought online – Photowall have a huge range of textures, from flaking plaster and paint, to brick walls and woodland scenes straight out of *A Midsummer's Nights Dream* (see Sources, pages 204–205). Some backdrops are huge and require a ladder to fix in place with special removable double-sided tape, while others are easy to roll up and transport. I have been known to carry them across the world in my suitcase when holding workshops abroad. They allow me to transform a blank studio wall into a magical flowery bower.

These backdrops and other props are essential to my work because they enable me to tell a story. I identify with them, and they make sense to me. It is important that your images and arrangements do the same for you. Use props if they feel right for your personal style. Experiment with backdrops if you want to create interesting texture or just to transport yourself to a fantasy world for a little while. But don't feel that you have to. It might be that a tall glass vase or a single beautiful ribbon is all that your perfect bouquet needs.

If you're taking images for a social media feed or a website, have a think about what you want your work to say about you and your personal brand. Do you want to capture a calm, clean, fresh feel? Something sparse, pared-back and minimal? Or are you in search of an image that is nostalgic and reflective of yesteryear? Whichever one it is, it's important to be consistent, stay true to yourself and, above all, create work that makes you happy.

MAKING JOURNALS
with natural ingredients

I'VE ALWAYS HAD A SLIGHTLY WORRYING OBSESSION FOR PAPER STATIONERY;
NOTEBOOKS IN PARTICULAR. MAYBE IT'S BECAUSE I ADORE BOOKS?

A NEW BOOK IS THE BIGGEST PLEASURE, and the thought of being able to tuck myself away somewhere quiet for a few hours while I pore over pages of inspiring images and wonderful words, evoking images of faraway places, thoughts and stories, keeps me cheerful even when the rain has defied all promises of the 'most waterproof coat' in the world and my clothes are definitely damp, if not soaking, after a day standing in a wet field planting trees.

And so I started to make and fill my own journals with stories of the passing seasons. I fill them with snippets of silk and linen from the dye pot and flowers cut from the garden and pressed between cartridge paper and heavy piles of old magazines. I make notes of exactly what went into the dye pot and stick in the notes as they did in old herbariums, and carefully fix the flower pressings in place with archival tape.

As well as these, I collect images, fragments of old wallpaper, sketches, clippings of floral fabric – anything that makes me curious and my heart sing. I sew these items in using old silver thread or dyed silks, using a running stitch, a stab stitch or French knots. My dressmaker mother taught me to sew and my grandmother to embroider and make patchwork quilts. I find the repetitious nature of stitching calming, and it forces me to focus on what is in front of me.

These journals become my muses and reconnect me to the natural landscape no matter what the season. In early summer, previous collections inspire new colour combinations in my floral work and inform my planting plans for the cutting garden. As the seasons progress, I can look back at my journal for a reminder of just how lovely that poppy was when the sun was at her brightest in early summer, and why it is important to collect and dry fallen rose petals throughout the summer to make beautiful dyes in autumn.

PAGES OF INSPIRATION
Winter is the perfect time for staying indoors and spending time focusing on the journals that I fill with silks, fabrics and flowers pressed and dried in the summer (opposite). They are an expression of my creative curiosity and allow me to pause for a while and be still in the moment.

I ignore the voice that tells me to start on the front page of a new journal and make sure that every page is beautiful, because I can never get past a blank first page. So I usually start a few pages in. I might work backwards, or I might not. It doesn't really matter. These journals aren't made to please anyone but me.

You will need

⁎ **A paper journal.** I buy deckle-edged journals that have been hand bound (see Sources, pages 204–205), but you could make your own paper and bind that.

⁎ **A large piece of paper** for a template

⁎ **Fabric to cover your journal.** I'm using a piece of silk that I dyed in summer from golden onion skins, but you can use anything that you love. The size will depend on your journal, but I would suggest a piece measuring approximately 30 x 30cm/12 x 12in.

⁎ **A pair of sharp fabric scissors**

⁎ **Fabric glue**

⁎ **Naturally dyed silk or velvet ribbon**

step 1

I lay the journal on a large piece of paper and draw around it to make a template for the cover, leaving a good 10cm/4in allowance. I pin this paper template to the fabric and cut around it, just like a dressmaking pattern. I apply a small quantity of good-quality fabric glue to the front cover and firmly press down the fabric, easing out any folds and creases. I apply more glue and cover the spine, then turn over and repeat on the back, gently stretching the fabric out. Don't apply too much glue, or it will seep through the fabric fibres and spoil the surface of the cloth. Leave to dry.

step 2

For a neat finish, turn the 10cm/4in fabric allowance over the edges and carefully glue it down before leaving to dry.

step 3

Personally, I prefer my journals to look slightly raw and unfinished, so I simply trim the excess fabric around the edges of the journal.

step 4

Finally, I choose a length of naturally dyed silk or velvet ribbon to wrap around my journal and tie in a bow. This keeps everything together as the contents grow.

READY AND WAITING
Wrapped in all her silken finery, my journal is all ready to go, with empty pages full of possibility (right).

A LASTING RECORD

This journal holds all the samples I take from the dye pot (above). By carefully recording my experiments with different plant dyes, I can either reproduce a colour fairly exactly or use it as a starting point for a new shade. I was dreadful at science at school, but this process fascinates me because the end results are so pretty. The vibrant orange at the top of the page was created by madder root dye, while the brown silk at the bottom was dyed with the same madder dye, then dipped into a very weak iron solution. The pale ointment pink shade on the same page was made with cutch (or catechu) extract, which comes from the acacia tree. The yellows and golds on the right-hand page were a careful mix of madder root and pomegranate, with the deep olive created from the application of another weak solution of iron.

CAPTURED BEAUTY

The pressed flower heads of *Papaver nudicaule* 'Champagne Bubbles', *Papaver rhoeas* 'Amazing Grey' and *Centaurea cyanus* 'Black Ball' are carefully removed from the flower press, then stuck into my journal using archival tape (left, below and overleaf). I insert a sheet of fine acid-free tissue paper between the pages to help preserve the flowers for as long as possible.

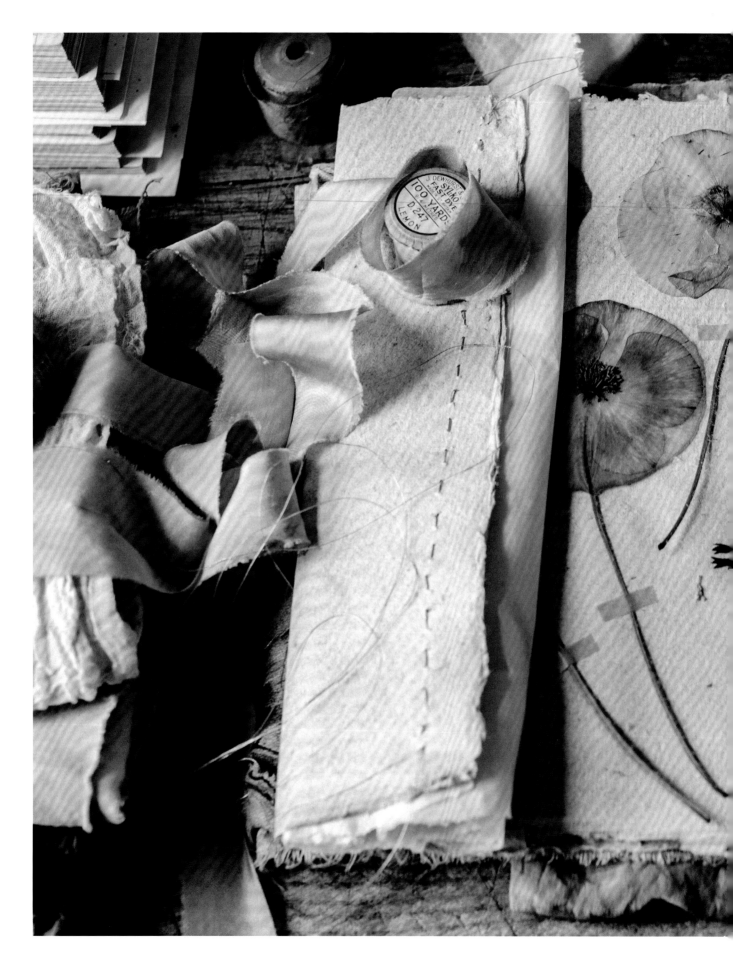

VINTAGE TREASURES

Apart from hand-dyed silks, my other obsession is vintage floral fabrics and wallpaper. Finding large pieces and rolls is difficult and can be expensive, but short lengths, just the perfect size for covering a journal, are more easily sourced from online antiques shops and auctions. Colour and pattern add variation to a stack of notebooks waiting to be filled and which are destined to become cherished objects in their own right (right). Old glass jars offer storage for silver threads and dyed silks wound around old bobbins and cotton reels.

THE EMOTIVE IMAGE

a tiny seasonal vase

THERE CAN BE SLIM PICKINGS IN THE GARDEN
DURING THE LONG MONTHS OF WINTER.

But you don't need a huge bunch of different flowers to put
together a joyous, mood-lifting little vase. As deepest winter
slowly moves past the New Year and starts to inch towards
spring, the first bulbs will start to emerge, and with fewer
flowers to choose from, those that do appear will seem all the
more precious and deserving of your attention. A tiny vase will
force you to choose your flowers with care, and every stem has
to earn her moment in the limelight.

TINY GEMS
To enhance this jewel box of winter bulbs, I choose a dark
background that will set off the delicate stems, and bring
in a feeling of warmth by dressing the table with a piece of
19th-century cotton floral fabric (left).

flowers and stems

✷ **Focal flowers x 5 or 6.** This will vary season to season, but look to see what is growing in the shade. I'm using *Narcissus* 'February Silver' and *N. bulbocodium* 'Arctic Bells', *Fritillaria uva-vulpis* and a few snowdrops.

✷ **Filler flowers x 1 or 2 stems.** The number of flowers depends on the size of your vase. I've chosen some *Helleborus foetidus* and a piece of dried limonium (statice) chosen for its colour.

You will need

✷ **A small glass vase or pot.** Even a small glass jam/jelly jar will work.

✷ **Floral snips**

✷ **Lazy Susan turntable**

step 1

Select your flowers. I'm using snowdrops, hellebores, narcissus and *Fritillaria uva-vulpis*. This last plant is commonly associated with spring, but I'm always impatient for its shy, nodding heads, so I usually pot a few bulbs up and bring them indoors in February to force into early flower. I also have a piece of limonium in a coral pink that will lift the colour palette.

step 2

Select your container. Anything will do as long as it holds water, but do consider the size of your flowers. Winter flowers such as snowdrops and hellebores tend to be slight and delicate, so will get lost in anything too big. Here, I'm using an antique Delft jar that's about 15cm/6in tall.

step 3

It is easier when working on a small scale to lift your container up to eye level. I'm using a paint tin with a Lazy Susan perched on top to give me a level surface and one I can easily turn. It means that I'm viewing the arrangement at the same height as my camera will capture later.

fritillaria uva-vulpis is one of my favourites.

step 4

Start with the bulkiest flowers first. The
hellebore has lovely hanging bells that I want
to drape over the rim. As the jar is small, the
hellebore stem will act as a support for the
other smaller stems, so I don't need to use any
tape or chicken wire.

step 5

I start to push in the snowdrops and
narcissus. I want to give them plenty of
room to breathe, so I have deliberately
kept the stems long.

step 6

I add more narcissus to give the arrangement height and push in the limonium at the back — I'm not interested in its form but its colour.

step 7

I add a fritillary on the right-hand side. It has grown long and leggy in the warmth of the house, and gives the arrangement a sense of whimsy.

step 8

I add a few more fritillaries, then some long-stemmed narcissus and I'm done. Place the finished vase where you can appreciate the flowers up close; they are jewels of the winter garden.

FLORIST SUPPLIES

New Covent Garden Market
Nine Elms Lane
London SW8 5NX
www.newcoventgardenmarket.com
*Wholesale flowers, foliage, plants
and sundries.*

Niwaki
www.niwaki.com
*For the best garden and flower snips and
Kenzan pin frog holders.*

San Francisco Flower Mart
640 Brannan Street
San Francisco, CA 94107
www.sanfranciscoflowermart.com
For wholesale flowers and all sundries.

Terrain
www.shopterrain.com
*USA-based chain of stores from the same
stable as Anthropologie, and offering
wonderful garden equipment, flower
snips and vases.*

PLANTS, FLOWERS & SEEDS

UK
Avon Bulbs
www.avonbulbs.co.uk
Instagram @botanical_tales
*A small family-run business supplying
quality bulbs and snowdrops in the green.*

C & K Jones International
www.jonestherose.co.uk
Instagram @jonestherose
Top quality bare-root and potted roses.

Chiltern Seeds
www.chilternseeds.co.uk
Instagram @chilternseeds
*A comprehensive online shop for
quality seeds.*
Rose Cottage Plants.
www.rosecottageplants.co.uk
Dahlia tubers and seasonal bulbs.

USA
Floret Flowers
www.floretflowers.com
*Heirloom seeds and tubers specializing
in unique and heirloom flowers.*

Heirloom Roses.
www.heirloomroses.com
Instagram @heirloom_roses
*A family-run business selling exquisite
roses for the garden.*

Rose Story Farm
www.rosestoryfarm.com
Instagram @rosestoryfarm
Field grown roses for wholesale and retail.

FLOWER FARMS & FRESH FLOWERS

Bluma Flower Farm
Joanna Letz
2201 Dwight Way
Berkeley, CA 94704
www.blumaflowerfarm.com
Instagram @blumafarm
*Local flower deliveries and pickup.
Workshops on flower farming and
arranging. Open by appointment only.*

Carol's Garden
www.carolsgarden.co.uk
Instagram @carolsiddorn
*Carol sells beautiful flowers from her
garden in Cheshire to both the public
and to wholesale florists. She also runs
workshops on growing and arranging.
Open by appointment only.*

Flowers from the Farm
www.flowersfromthefarm.co.uk
Instagram @flowersfromthefarm
*An extensive list of all the flower farmers
and growers in the UK.*

The Real Flower Company
www.realflowers.co.uk
Instagram @therealflowerco
*Award-winning English growers and
wholesalers of garden roses and seasonal
flowers, including for home delivery.*

Slow Flowers
www.slowflowers.com
Instagram @slowflowerssociety
*An online directory of florists, studio
designers, wedding and event planners
and flower farmers committed to using
US and Canadian-grown flowers.*

Usk Valley Roses
www.uskvalleyroses.co.uk
Instagram @uskvalleyroses
British-grown scented garden roses.

DRIED FLOWERS

Botanical Tales
www.botanicaltales.com
Instagram @botanical_tales
*Everlasting dried botanical displays and
wreaths by floral artist Bex Partridge.*

Just Dahlias
www.justdahlias.co.uk
Instagram @justdahlias
*Dahlias both fresh and dried. Dahlias can
be tricky to dry, but Philippa Stewart does
it beautifully and will send nationwide.*

FABULOUS PROPS & BACKDROPS

Chloe Cyphus Antiques
www.chloeantiques.com
*Beautiful French and Swedish antiques,
props and urns. Delivery worldwide.*

Gaia
www.gaiavessels.com
*Ceramic vessels created by floral designers;
perfect for weddings and events.*

Garden Brocante
www.gardenbrocante.etsy.com
*UK-based seller of antique garden pots
and urns for bulbs and planting.*

Maison Artefact
273 Lillie Road
London SW6 7LL
www.maisonartefact.com
*Swedish and French antiques, garden
furniture and urns. Delivery worldwide.*

Nikki Page Antiques
www.nikkipageantiques.com
Decorative French antiques and urns.
Delivery worldwide.

No.44 Permillion
www.permillion44.com
Vintage props and flower presses.
International delivery available.

Photowall
instagram @photowall_sweden
www.photowall.co.uk
For a huge selection of mural backdrops
in bespoke sizes to fit your wall.

SILK & ORGANIC LINENS FOR DYEING

Aurora Silk
www.aurorasilk.com
Beautiful organic silks for natural dyeing.
Delivery worldwide.

Botanical Inks
www.botanicalinks.com
Organic peace silk and undyed knitting
yarn as well as naturally dyed yarn. Also
workshops on using natural dyes.

Botanical Colors.
www.botanicalcolors.com
Textiles for dyeing as well as seeds so you
can grow your own plants for dyeing.
Delivery worldwide.

Etsy
www.etsy.com
An excellent worldwide resource for old,
antique and vintage French linen.

Wild Colours
www.wildcolours.co.uk
UK-based company providing natural
dyes, dye extracts, mordants, modifers
and useful information on natural dyeing.
Delivery worldwide.

NATURALLY DYED SILK RIBBONS

Heirloom Silk
www.heirloomsilk.com
Silk ribbons dyed by hand using flowers
grown in Somerset. Will ship worldwide.

The Natural Dye Works
Ros Humphries
instagram @thenaturaldyeworks
www.thenaturaldyeworks.com
Exquisite silk ribbons dyed from naturally
foraged flowers plus workshops on
natural dyeing.

Silk and Willow
www.silkandwillow.com
US website offering naturally dyed silk
and chiffon ribbons and table linens,
handmade paper goods and antiques.

ART MATERIALS

Case for Making
www.caseformaking.com
Instagram @caseformaking
Lose yourself for hours in this San
Francisco art shop. Paints, ceramic
palettes, papers and workshops.
Delivers internationally.

Green and Stone
251–253 Fulham Road
London SW3 6HY
www.greenandstone.com
Instagram @greenandstone
A treasure trove of everything you could
possibly desire to create your masterpiece.

Jacksons Art
www.jacksonsart.com
Instagram @jacksons_art
A comprehensive selection of artists'
supplies and unstretched canvas on the
roll to buy by the metre.

PAPER & JOURNALS

Khadi Papers
www.khadi.com
Instagram @khadipapers
Handmade papers and journals.

Saint Signora
www.saintsignora.com
Instagram @saintsignora
A wonderful online treasure trove that
sells small antiques as well as handmade
paper goods and journals.

PODCASTS

The Restless Creatives
www.therestlesscreatives.co.uk
A weekly podcast chatting to makers,
artisans and other creatives about their
inspirations, influences and challenges.

Botanical Brouhaha
www.botanicalbrouhaha.com
Instagram @botanicalbrouhaha
A podcast for flower lovers.

GARDENS TO VISIT & PLACES TO STAY

Broadfield Court
Bowley Lane
Hereford HR1 3LG
www.broadfieldcourt.com
Instagram @broadfield_court
An historic country house and wedding
venue set in beautiful gardens and
grounds. Available for private hire.

The Laundry Garden
The Laundry
Llanrhaeadr
North Wales LL16 4NL
www.thelaundryretreatnorthwales.co.uk
Instagram @thelaundrygarden
B&B accommodation and log cabins plus
an old walled garden.

Middleton Lodge
Kneeton Lane
Middleton Tyas
Richmond
North Yorkshire DL10 6NJ
www.middletonlodge.co.uk
Instagram @middletonlodge
A Georgian country retreat with a kitchen
garden designed by Tom Stuart Smith.
.
Newby Hall & Gardens
Ripon
North Yorkshire HG4 5AE
www.newbyhall.com
Instagram @newbyhallandgardens
Country house and garden open to visitors
and available for weddings and event hire.

Index

Page numbers in *italic* refer to the illustrations

Thanks

Writing a book has been one of the hardest yet most wonderful things I've ever attempted, and there are so many people who have helped to make it possible. I owe huge thanks to Rachel Ashwell for introducing me to my publisher Cindy Richards, and to Cindy for taking a punt on me and saying yes.

Thank you to Annabel Morgan and Leslie Harrington at RPS, for pulling all my random thoughts together in such an effortlessly beautiful way, as well as head of production Patricia Harrington.

Thanks also to Gabriela, for opening my eyes to a whole world of possibilities and wonderful friendship and to Max, for your endless creative genius.

I'm eternally grateful to my lovely friends Brigitte and Fiona for putting up with my wittering and angst for months on end, and my dear friend Vicks, whose gentle and wise encouragement (along with the occasional large glass of wine) has kept me vaguely sane and focused.

Thank you to Carol, to whom I owe a huge debt of gratitude for her exquisite flowers that make bringing the outside in so easy, and to Jenny, Rebecca and Joanna, for opening up their beautiful gardens where I can lose myself with my camera.

Thank you to Mum and Dad, for your never-ending love and support and many other things I don't have room to write, to Sylvie, for being the best sister and setting me on this flowery path, and to Matthew, who will always be the teenager.

Finally, and most importantly, a world of thanks and love to my husband Richard, who keeps the wheels turning and always makes me laugh, even when my creative streak feels as if it's gone on holiday without me.

LUCY HUNTER has a fine art degree and more than 20 years' experience working as an award-winning landscape designer, floral artist and self-taught photographer. Passionate about seasonal flowers, gardens and the natural landscape, Lucy is constantly exploring ways to soften the boundaries between inside and out, capturing transitory shifts in nature and the seasons. She lives in North Wales with her husband, teenager and dogs, and holds workshops across the world on floral design, composing the perfect image and finding your creative voice. Find her on Instagram @lucytheflowerhunter.